Introduction: Studying History and Passing Exams

History is a mystery – and solving it can be great fun!

Learning about the past involves detective work. In order to know and understand events from years gone by, how people lived, what they thought and did, you have to try to solve a whole series of puzzles – some much more complicated than others.

To find out about history, especially the recent past, you probably started by asking parents, grandparents, teachers. For most of the more distant past you have to use a wider variety of evidence to build a picture you can see and understand. Part of the detective work involves finding relevant sources of evidence and then trying to fit these together to make as clear and accurate a picture as you can.

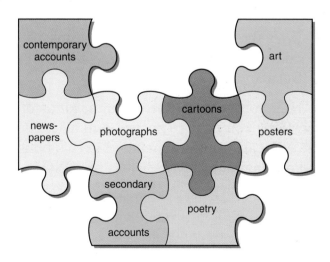

The Jigsaw of Evidence

Each of the pieces in the jigsaw is valuable but as you can see the jigsaw is not complete. This is a problem which faces all historians! Usually you have to try to see the past using only some of the evidence you might like to have. In this book you will find many types of historical evidence such as:

◆ written personal accounts,

◆ official records,

◆ quotations from other history books,

◆ newspaper and magazine extracts,

◆ letters, poetry, memoirs,

◆ pictures, cartoons, photographs, maps.

You can use these to help you reconstruct and understand the past but there is other evidence which cannot go into a book, such as films, artefacts (clothes, tools, weapons) and archaeological evidence. The more evidence you can use and the more skilfully you can use it, the better and more accurate will be your picture of the past!

Using evidence and passing examinations

There are several different things you can do with historical evidence. You can use it to gain KNOWLEDGE and UNDERSTANDING [KU] or to make an ENQUIRY. [ENQ]

◆ You can use evidence to describe something, such as why a war started, what someone did, how important an invention was. [KU]

◆ You can use it to decide what the person or persons who produced it thought or wanted others to think. [ENQ]

◆ You can compare pieces of evidence to see if they agree or disagree or to help you reach your own conclusions. [ENQ]

◆ You can make up your own mind about the value of evidence, based on such things as WHEN it was produced, WHY it was produced, HOW it was produced and WHO produced it. [ENQ].

Not many people like sitting Examinations. Yet an examination, especially one set and marked by people who do not know you, is a very good way for you to prove what you can do. Most people train and prepare better when they know there is a game or race or test at the end! Books like this help your training by building your knowledge and skills and confidence. Here are some suggestions to help you succeed.

◆ Remember the examination is meant to give you an opportunity to show what you can do. It is NOT full of traps and tricks to find out what you cannot do. Both you and the examiners know what topics you have been studying and the examination will be based on some of these. Sources will be like ones you have used – they may even be the same in some cases!

◆ When you sit an examination look carefully for the contexts you have studied and answer ONLY those ones.

◆ Read sources and questions carefully to decide what it is you are asked to do. AND look at he number of marks for each question to help you decide how much to write in your answer, so that you do not waste time writing too much.

◆ Never copy a whole source almost word for word into an answer, because this does not show that you understand or can use the source.

Questions like the following are asking you to show your **Knowledge and Understanding [KU]** of the past.

◆ What changes happened in Skye around 1840?

◆ Describe some of the dangers workers faced in coalmines in the 1840s.

◆ Why did war break out in Europe in 1914?

◆ How important was militarism to Nazi rule in Germany?

You are expected to use your **Enquiry [ENQ]** skills when you see the following,

◆ How useful is the source in explaining why changes happened in Skye around 1840?

◆ Do the sources agree about the dangers workers faced in coalmines in the 1840s?

◆ How fully does the source explain the outbreak of war in 1914?

◆ Does the author of the source think militarism was important to Nazi rule in Germany?

To help you, more of the different kinds of questions you have to answer and activities you can carry out are included in this book and are marked as either [KU] or [ENQ].

Good luck with any examinations that you sit. But if you follow the advice above, and use this book thoughtfully and carefully, then you shouldn't need any luck – and you should enjoy solving the many mysteries of history . . .

1 The End of the Reich

Defeat for the army

1918 was a bad year in which to be German. True, it started well enough. In March, the war in the east came to an end when the new **Bolshevik** government in Russia signed the Treaty of Brest-Litovsk. Suddenly, Germany had a million extra soldiers to fight in the west.

General Ludendorff's new storm troops broke out of the trenches that had held the armies for almost four years. They drove the British and French back so quickly that it seemed they might take Paris. Germany might have won the war before American reinforcements could help the Allies. Then, just as had happened in 1914, they were stopped and turned back at the river Marne.

Ludendorff called 8 August 1918, 'the black day of the Germany Army'. The Allies counter-attacked, supported by 3400 big guns and 600 tanks. For the next two months they pushed the Germans back towards the Rhine. German soldiers lost heart.

The soldiers of the countries allied to Germany were also tired of the war. In September and October 1918 Germany's allies Bulgaria, Turkey and Austria surrendered.

By early October the generals, Ludendorff and Hindenburg, knew that the war was lost. They decided to ask the Allies to stop fighting.

The suffering of the people

Throughout the war the German people had suffered greatly. German food production fell badly because so many farm workers had to join the army. German industry, short of raw materials, found it hard enough to supply the army, let alone the needs of the people. Worse, the British navy blockaded Germany, stopping goods from reaching port. By 1918 everything – food, clothing, fuel – was in short supply. Workers went on strike to support their demand for shorter working hours. They did this because they found it hard to work with so little to eat.

To make things even worse, a virus called Spanish 'flu hit Germany as it did other European countries. Over 400 000 people died from this virus and from food shortages before the end of the year. Ordinary Germans became desperate. Many of them simply wanted the war to end. Many of them felt they could not trust their country's leaders any more. Look at Source 1.2 to see how much worse off people in Germany and Austria were compared to those in Britain.

> **Source 1.1** Ludendorff, 'My War Memoirs'
>
> *I was told of behaviour which I should not have thought possible in the German Army; whole bodies of men had surrendered to single troopers. Retiring troops, meeting a fresh division going bravely into action, had shouted out things like "Blackleg" and "You're prolonging the war".*

Source 1.2   'Illustrated London News', March 1918

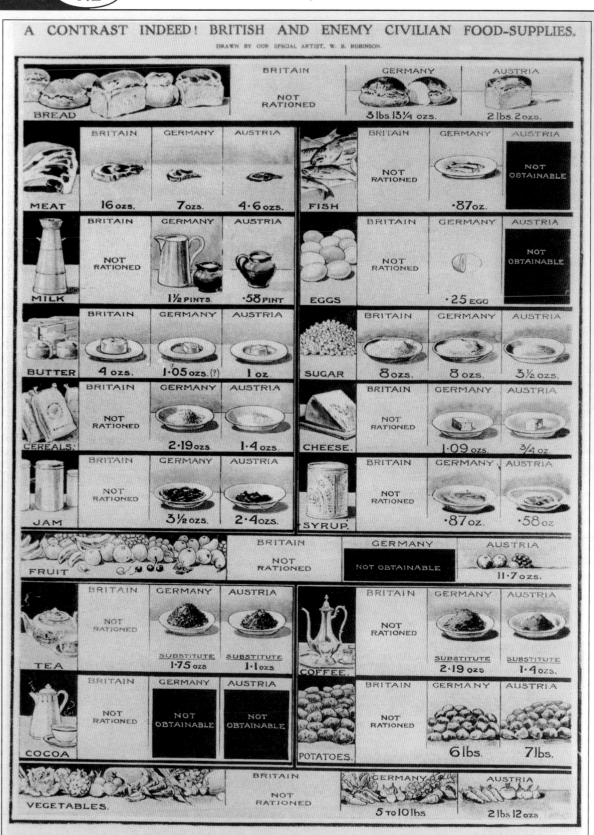

A CONTRAST INDEED! BRITISH AND ENEMY CIVILIAN FOOD-SUPPLIES.

DRAWN BY OUR SPECIAL ARTIST, W. B. ROBINSON.

THE FOOD SITUATION IN THIS COUNTRY COMPARED WITH THAT IN GERMANY AND AUSTRIA: RELATIVE RATIONS AND SUPPLIES (OR ABSENCE THEREOF) SHOWN IN DIAGRAM.

Those inclined to grumble at the minor inconveniences—in no sense, privations—caused by our rationing system would do well to read, mark, learn, and inwardly "digest" these diagrams, which indicate the far greater shortage of food to which the Germans and Austrians have been subjected. In all cases except sugar, where the British and German rations are the same, the quantities of the various foods available to our enemies are much less than our own. Some articles of food are not obtainable at all in Germany or Austria. As regards the German butter ration of 1·05 oz., it is doubtful whether this includes margarine. The British ration of 4 oz. includes both. The tea and coffee available in the enemy countries is of the "substitute" variety. The plates in the diagrams have been drawn to a scale of 6 inches diameter.—[Drawing Copyrighted in the United States and Canada.]

Source **1.3** Starving Germans being forced from a potato field where they have been scavenging for something to eat

Activities

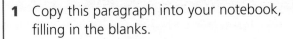

1 Copy this paragraph into your notebook, filling in the blanks.

   1918 started well for _____. _____ fell out of the war, so Germany had a _____ more soldiers to fight in the _____. When they attacked there, the _____ advanced almost to _____ before being stopped at the river _____. **(KU)**

2 Read Source 1.1. Why was Ludendorff shocked by the behaviour of Germany soldiers in the last months of the war? Give two reasons. **(KU)**

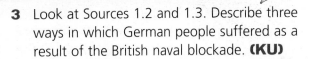

3 Look at Sources 1.2 and 1.3. Describe three ways in which German people suffered as a result of the British naval blockade. **(KU)**

4 Why is Source 1.3 useful as evidence about the lives of German people at the end of the war? Give two reasons. **(ENQ)**

5 Source 1.2 was published in Britain in March 1918.

   a) What message do you think it was trying to give to its British readers? **(ENQ)**

   b) Why might it **not** be reliable as evidence about food supplies in Germany? **(ENQ)**

6 Why, by October 1918, did many Germans want the war to end? Give as many reasons as you can. **(KU)**

The fall of the Kaiser

Kaiser Wilhelm II and the generals had led Germany throughout the war. When they realised that it had been lost, the army leaders did not want to be the ones to make peace. This was because

◆ they did not want to accept the blame for losing the war

◆ they hoped that a civilian government might get a better deal from the Allies

◆ they wanted to save the army's reputation, so that it would still be important after the war

◆ they hoped a civilian government might help the Kaiser to keep his throne.

On 3 October 1918 Prince Max of Baden became Chancellor. He was shocked to find out how near Germany was to defeat, as the generals had kept this secret. He asked the Allies for an armistice. **President Wilson** of the USA insisted that the government leaders would first have to resign and that the Kaiser would have to give up his throne. This was because the Allies blamed the Kaiser personally for the death and destruction of the war. They would not deal with him.

There were also problems inside Germany. On 28 October sailors at Wilhelmshaven were ordered to sea for a last, desperate attack on the British navy. They refused and took up arms against the government, as you can see in the photograph Source 1.4. This was mutiny and it was followed by another at Keil on 3 and 4 November. Although the soldiers in the army remained loyal, these naval revolts were followed by uprisings in cities all over Germany. Workers' and Soldiers' Councils (*Räte*) were set up to run local government. These rebellions showed the strength of the demand for peace across the whole country. For a time, it seemed that Germany might even have a Communist revolution like the one in Russia in 1917.

Source 1.4 Sailors taking part in the mutiny

Source 1.5 — Colonel Hans von Haeften, reporting Ebert's speech

The people were widely convinced that the Kaiser was the guilty one. The main thing was that the people wanted to see the man they held responsible for the disaster removed from his post. The abdication of the Kaiser was absolutely necessary to prevent revolution.

The threats from both outside and inside Germany made the government decide that there was only one way out. On 6 November Friedrich Ebert, leader of the Social Democratic Party (SPD), spoke to army leaders.

Three days later huge crowds marched on the government buildings in Berlin. Prince Max announced that the Kaiser had abdicated. At the same time the Prince resigned to let Ebert become Chancellor. Later that day, the Kaiser fled to Holland. The monarchy was finished. To stop them becoming violent, one of Ebert's supporters, Philipp Scheidemann, told the crowds in Berlin that Germany had become a republic.

On 11 November the armistice with the Allies was signed and the fighting came to an end. For Ebert, the problem was now to keep control in Germany. This would not be easy.

Activities

1 Why did the generals give up power to civilians? Give at least four reasons. **(KU)**

2 How valuable is Source 1.4 as evidence about the sailor's mutiny of November 1914? **(ENQ)**

3 Read Source 1.5. What did Ebert fear would happen if the Kaiser stayed?

4 Discuss the value of Source 1.5 as evidence about the political state of Germany on November 1918. **(ENQ)**

5 How fully does Source 1.5 explain why the Kaiser lost his throne in 1918? You should mention events inside and outside Germany in your answer. **(ENQ)**

2 The German Revolution

The Spartacist revolt

Ebert found himself at the head of a country in chaos. Many towns and cities were ruled by Workers' or Soldiers' Councils. Some of these just wanted to keep the peace and support law and order. Others wanted the revolution to go much further. They wanted the government to break the power of the army. They also wanted it to take over industry and land, and run them for the people. This is called Socialism.

Ebert was a Socialist as well, but he wanted these things to come about gradually, by people voting for them. Those who wanted them to happen quickly, through violent revolution, were called Communists, or 'Reds'. Already, they had taken over some cities.

Source	2.1	Ministry of War report, 8 November 1918

5 p.m.: Halle and Leipzig Red. Evening: Düsseldorf, Halstein, Osnabrück, Lauenburg Red; Magdeburg, Stuttgart, Oldenburg, Brunswick and Cologne all Red.

Ebert needed help. On 9 November, the day of the uprising in Berlin, he met General Wilhelm Groener, the army Chief of Staff. They agreed that the army would support the new government. In return, the government would fight against Communism.

The Communists were angry that Ebert's government did not follow Socialist

Source	2.2	Armed Spartacists march in Berlin

policies. They accused him of betraying the working classes. On 6 January 1919 a band of Communists calling themselves the Spartacus League, led by Karl Liebknecht and Rosa Luxemburg, rose in Berlin. They became known as the **Spartacists**.

They called a general strike. They took over important buildings, including newspaper offices, railway stations and even a brewery. They put up barriers and stood guard in some of the main streets.

The *Freikorps*

The government needed more help than the army could give. There were others they could turn to. Some men who had been officers in the army were left with no jobs

Source 2.3 *Freikorps* soldiers in Berlin

when the army was reduced in size. They hated what had been done to Germany and to the army. They also hated Communism. These men began to form small volunteer groups called *Freikorps* (Free Corps), with some help from the government. They gathered uniforms and weapons, including field guns, machine guns and even armoured cars.

Gustav Noske, the Defence Minister, raised an army from these *Freikorps* to march on Berlin. On 11 January he led them into the centre of the city himself. They began by using artillery to capture the police headquarters from the rebels.

Over the next four days the Freikorps defeated the rebels and took control of the city. Then they hunted down the Spartacist leaders. Liebknecht and Luxemburg were arrested and murdered the same night by *Freikorps* officers. The revolt was over, but many working class people never forgave the government for putting it down.

Activities

1 Germany had become a republic. What other changes did some Socialists want to happen? **(KU)**

2 What did Ebert and the Communists

   a) agree about?

   b) disagree about? **(KU)**

3 a) Look at Source 2.1. What evidence is there that Communists were a serious threat in many parts of Germany? **(KU)**

   b) Give two reasons why Source 2.2 is useful as evidence about the Spartacist rising in Berlin. **(ENQ)**

4 Here are some sentences. Copy them into your notebook in the correct order to tell the story of the Spartacist revolt in Berlin.

◆ The Defence Minister led the Freikorps into the city.

◆ The Spartacist leaders, Karl Liebknecht and Rosa Luxemburg, were killed.

◆ The Spartacus League took over important buildings and called a general strike.

◆ The Government collected an army of Freikorps, volunteer groups of soldiers.

◆ Within four days the rebellion collapsed.

◆ The Freikorps used artillery and machine guns to defeat the rebels. **(KU)**

5 Were the Spartacists defeated because they had poorer weapons than the Freikorps? Use Sources 2.2 and 2.3 and your own knowledge to come to a conclusion. **(KU)**

The left divided

Before 1914 the Social Democratic Party had been strong. The outbreak of war divided the Socialists – some wanted to support the war effort, but others thought that working-class people should refuse to fight each other. In 1917 they split from the majority to form the Independent Socialist Party (USPD). They were important enough, and still close enough to the SPD in their aims, for **Ebert** to bring them into his government. The cabinet included three members each from the SPD and the Independent Socialists.

It proved difficult for the two groups to work together as they had different priorities:

◆ Ebert and the Majority Socialists in the SPD wanted to bring Germany back to normal life after the turmoil of war and revolution. They looked at the experience of Russia after the Bolshevik revolution. Its economy was in ruins, many of its people were starving and the country was in the middle of a terrible civil war. They were terrified that Germany might suffer the same fate if they failed to restore stability quickly. This was why they were willing to work with the army and the old civil service, but this policy brought them into conflict with the USPD.

◆ The Independent Socialists thought that this was their one chance to turn Germany into a socialist country, in which large-scale industry would be run by the state for the benefit of ordinary people. If these radical changes did not come with the revolution, they might never come at all. This explains their anger at Ebert's refusal to give the introduction of Socialism a higher priority.

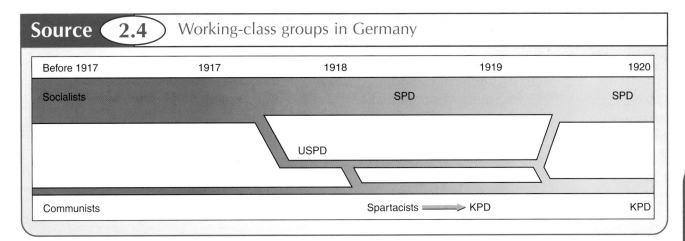

Source 2.4 Working-class groups in Germany

In December 1918, a national congress of Workers' and Soldiers' Councils met in Berlin. It agreed that there should be an elected National Assembly to decide the future government of Germany. Before elections could be held, disagreements inside the cabinet led to the resignation of the Independent Socialists. Shortly afterwards, the Spartacists formed the German Communist Party (KPD). Now there were three groups, all claiming to represent the German working class.

The government's reaction

Both the Independent Socialists and the Communists accused the government of making too many compromises with the old Germany: the army, the civil service and big business. They argued that Ebert and his colleagues had betrayed the working class.

The government's reaction to the Spartacist revolt finally split the left. In fact, the rising was so badly led that it had no hope of success, as the Communists' own newspaper saw.

Source 2.5 **Die Rote Fahne** (The Red Flag)

Proletarians were standing shoulder to shoulder . . . They were ready to do anything, give anything, even their lives . . .

The masses were standing from nine in the morning in the cold and fog. Somewhere their leaders were sitting and conferring. Noon came and, in addition to the cold, hunger came. And the leaders conferred . . . The fog came again and with it the dusk. The masses went home sad. They wanted great things but they had done nothing. Because their leaders conferred.

What horrified the revolutionaries most was that it was a government, whose members claimed to be on the side of the working classes, which used force against them. First, the Defence Minister himself led the *Freikorps* against the revolutionaries in Berlin. In the spring of 1919 they were used again in Berlin and in Munich.

Their methods were often brutal. Over a thousand people, many of them innocent civilians who had nothing to do with the revolution, were killed as the risings were put down.

The use of these units seemed to prove that Ebert had abandoned the workers. Yet it was hard for him to find an alternative if he was to avoid complete chaos. His main priority was to help Germany cope with the aftermath of war and to return to some kind of normal life. To him, Germany in 1919 needed stability more than it needed Socialism.

Democracy in Germany

The long-term effects of these events were tragic for democracy in Germany. In future,

the Communists detested the SPD for their actions. The two parties fought each other so hard that they divided the working-class vote at elections, and they were unable to act together against those who would become their real enemies on the right, the Nazis. In this way the German republic lost from the start one of its most important defences, the support of the class which created it.

Source 2.6 A *Freikorps* unit and artillery in Berlin, April 1919

Activities

1   Explain in your own words the reasons for the disagreements between the Independent Socialists **(USPD)** and the Majority Socialists **(SPD). (KU)**

2   Do you think the writer of Source 2.5 approved of the Spartacist leaders? Give reasons for your opinion. **(ENQ)**

3   What decoration has been added to the Freikorps armoured cars in Sourced 2.6 and what does this suggest about members of the Freikorps? **(KU)**

4   Compare the evidence about the Freikorps in Sources 2.3 and 2.6. **(ENQ)**

5   How important was weak leadership as a reason for the failure of the Spartacist revolt? Use the evidence in the sources and your own knowledge to support your conclusion. **(KU)**

3 The Peace Settlement

Making the treaty

Once the Kaiser and military government had gone, many Germans believed that the Allies no longer had a quarrel with the German people. They thought the new government would help make the peace treaty. They were wrong. They thought the peace treaty would be based on President Wilson's 'Fourteen Points', which had been offered to Germany as a basis for peace in 1917. They were wrong again. The Allies wrote the treaty and told the Germans to sign or face invasion.

When they saw the treaty, the Germans were horrified. Some even wanted to fight on and be crushed rather than accept the humiliating terms in the treaty. They called it the *Diktat* – the dictated peace. The government knew that Germany could not fight on. To do so would cause unbearable suffering to the German people. On 28 June 1919 the treaty was signed in the Hall of Mirrors in the Palace of Versailles near Paris. A British official described the occasion.

Source 3.1 Harold Nicolson, 'Peacemaking 1919'

Through the doors at the end come four officers of France, Great Britain, America and Italy. And then, isolated and pitiable, come the two Germans, Dr Müller, Dr Bell. The silence is terrifying. They keep their eyes fixed away from those 2000 staring eyes, fixed upon the ceiling. They are deathly pale. There is general tension. They sign. There is general relaxation. We kept our seats while the Germans were conducted like prisoners from the dock.

What the treaty said

The treaty they signed punished the Germans in several ways.

◆ Germany lost land to Belgium and to the new country of Poland. She also had to return Alsace and Lorraine to France.

Source 3.2 The signing of the Treaty of Versailles. Note how grand the hall is.

◆ All of Germany's overseas colonies were taken away.

The treaty also tried to make sure that Germany would never again have the strength to fight another war.

◆ The German army was to be limited to only 100 000 men.

◆ Germany was to have no air force or submarines.

◆ No German soldiers or weapons were allowed to be placed near the border with France.

Sources 3.3 and 3.4 show what land Germany was forced to surrender in 1919.

Source 3.4 Germany in 1919

Source 3.3 Germany in 1914

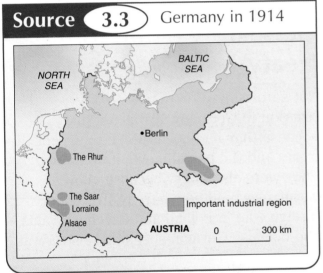

These terms forced on Germany were bad enough because they took so much from Germany and left her almost defenceless, but other points seemed to be meant as insults.

◆ By the 'War Guilt' clause, Germany had to accept the blame for starting the war.

◆ Because of this, Germany had to pay reparations. This meant they were to pay to repair the damage done to French and Belgian property during the war.

◆ All the coal mined in the Saar region of Germany was to go to France for the next 15 years.

FOUNDATION/GENERAL LEVEL

Activities

1 Why did the Germans expect to take part in drawing up the treaty? Give at least two reasons. **(KU)**

2 Look at Sources 3.1 and 3.2.

a) What evidence in Source 3.1 suggests that many people in the Hall were not certain that the Germans would sign? **(ENQ)**

b Compare the evidence about the treatment of the Germans in the two sources. **(ENQ)**

3 Which points in the treaty were meant to:

◆ make it hard for Germany to fight another war

◆ punish Germany

◆ make it seem right that Germany should be punished? **(KU)**

4 Look at Sources 3.3 and 3.4. Was the treaty likely to damage the German economy? **(KU)**

Group discussion
A treaty can be thought of as good if it helps to keep peace in the future. Draw up lists of what your group thinks were good points about the settlement and bad points about the settlement for keeping the peace. Does your group think the treaty was a fair one or not? Give as many reasons as you can for your decision.

13

Arguments over the treaty

Even while it was being drawn up the treaty was the subject of debate. The three leaders who were responsible for it had very different outlooks.

President Woodrow Wilson of the USA would have liked a peace settlement that was not too harsh. He wanted to be known as the man who brought a lasting peace to Europe. In contrast, **Georges Clemenceau** of France had a single practical aim. He was determined that Germany should be crushed so completely that France need never again fear invasion. The British Prime Minister, David Lloyd George, was caught between his own wish to be fair and the British people's feelings, summed up in phrases like 'hang the Kaiser', 'make Germany pay' and 'squeeze them until the pips squeak'. As the conference was held in the very emotional atmosphere of Paris, there was no doubt which view would win.

When the treaty was published, even some of the Allies were shocked. The American Secretary of State, Robert Lansing, wrote:

Source **3.5**	Memorandum, Robert Lansing

*The impression made by it is one of disappointment, of regret, and of depression. The terms of peace appear immeasurably harsh and humiliating, while many of them seem to be impossible of performance. The **League [of Nations]** as now constituted will be the prey of greed and intrigue.*

In contrast, Lloyd George told the British Parliament what he thought the treaty had achieved.

Source **3.6**	Lloyd George's speech to the House of Commons, 21 July 1919

We have disarmed; we have punished. We have demonstrated, I think, to the world that you cannot trample on national rights and liberties, that you cannot break covenants . . .

This is the task which we set ourselves, and I claim that this Treaty will be a lighthouse in the deep, warning nations and the rulers of nations against the perils against which the German Empire shattered itself.

German reaction to the treaty

Not surprisingly, there was an angry reaction in Germany. It was not just because they had been forced to accept the treaty and the punishments it contained. They were also angry because many Germans would now have to live under foreign rule in Poland and Czechoslovakia, and because German-speaking Austria was not allowed to join with Germany.

This anger showed itself quickly. The *Deutsche Zeitung* (German News) spoke for many on the day the treaty was signed. A black mourning band surrounded the main article.

Source 3.7 'Deutsche Zeitung', 28 June 1919

*VENGEANCE!
GERMAN NATION!*

Today in the Hall of Mirrors at Versailles, a disgraceful treaty is being signed. Never forget it! On that spot where, in the glorious year of 1871, the German Empire in all its glory began, today German honour is dragged to the grave. Never forget it! The German people with unceasing labour, will push forward to reconquer that place among nations to which they are entitled. Then there will be vengeance for the shame of 1919.

Writing in exile in Holland, the Kaiser made a similar forecast about the future.

Source 3.9 Kaiser Wilhelm II, Memoirs

After years of the heaviest trial will come the liberation from a yoke imposed unjustly upon a great, strong, honest nation. Then every one of us will be glad and proud that he is a German.

The impact on Germany

There has been much debate over both the fairness and wisdom of the Treaty of Versailles. Its terms appeared likely to have dreadful effects on a German economy

Source 3.8 Germany 1919. The shaded areas show where German speaking people lived outside Germany

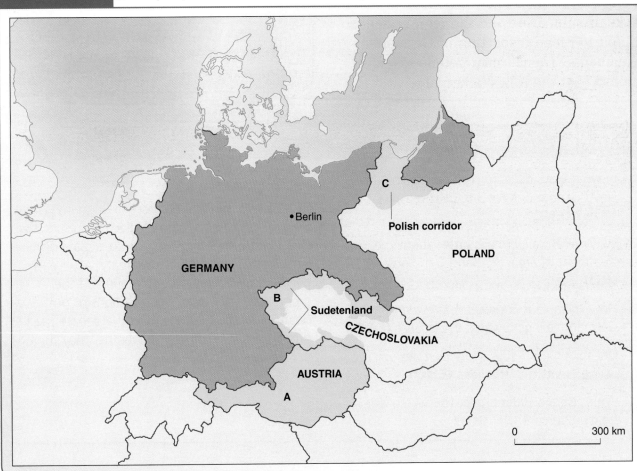

GENERAL/CREDIT LEVEL

already weakened by the war. The loss of population, the division of East Prussia from the rest of Germany by the 'Polish Corridor', the removal of overseas colonies, the loss of industrial production and, most of all, the crippling burden of reparations all suggested this would be the case. In fact, the colonies were almost worthless anyway, and the damage to the structure of the economy turned out to be temporary, despite the horrors of the inflation of 1922–1923 (see Chapter 6). By 1927, Germany was actually producing more industrial goods than she had done in 1913.

The military terms of the treaty had a much greater impact on Germany. It was not just that the army was reduced to 100 000 men, a number regarded by some people as too small even to defend the country against trouble inside its own borders. It was not even the refusal to allow Germany to have tanks or submarines, or the requirement to submit to Allied inspection of German armaments. The German people resented the fact that the Allies talked of

disarmament but only Germany was forced to disarm. They resented the Allied policy of 'national self determination of peoples' – the idea that people who were seen as national groups should be allowed to have their own countries – which led to the creation of new countries such as Czechoslovakia and Poland. It seemed that only Germans were to be denied this 'self determination'. Along with the hated War Guilt clause, these humiliations hurt the Germans very deeply. They gave **Adolf Hitler** an easy theme with which to gain the support of the German people.

> **Source 3.10**   **Adolf Hitler**, 'Mein Kampf'
>
> *Each one of the points of that Treaty could be branded in the minds and hearts of the German people until 60 million men and women find their souls aflame with a feeling of rage and shame; and a torrent of fire bursts forth as from a furnace, and a will of steel is forged from it, with the common cry – "we will have arms again!"*

Activities

1 In what ways did Lansing (Source 3.5) and Lloyd George (Source 3.6) disagree about the treaty? **(ENQ)**

2 Why were the Germans bitter about the treatment of areas A, B and C in Source 3.8? **(KU)**

3 How valuable is Source 3.7 as evidence of German feelings towards the treaty? **(ENQ)**

4 Does Source 3.7 fully show German opinion of the Treaty of Versailles? **(ENQ)**

5 What use did Hitler expect to make of the treaty (Source 3.10)? **(KU)**

Debate

Choose four pupils to represent Germany, Great Britain, France and the USA. Each representative should prepare a short speech to explain his or her country's opinion of the treaty. After each person has spoken, other members of the group/class may ask them questions or put points to them. At the end of the debate the group/class should vote on whether they think the treaty was a fair one.

4 The Weimar Republic

A new constitution

On 19 January 1919, 30 million Germans voted for the members of the National Assembly. The newly-elected Assembly met just over a fortnight later in the small city of Weimar in the middle of Germany. The meeting was held there because there was still a danger of violence in Berlin.

The Assembly's job was to write a new constitution for Germany. This would say how governments would be elected, what their powers would be and what rights people would have.

Source **4.1** Weimar. The quiet city was connected more with poetry than with politics

Source 4.2 — Opening speech by Ebert to the National Assembly, 6 February 1919

So we shall go to work with our grand aim firmly before us, to defend and protect the rights of the German people, to build a strong democracy in Germany and to fill it with true social spirit and socialistic deed. . . . We want to build a Reich of justice and truth, based upon the equality of all human beings.

First, the Assembly elected Ebert as President of the new German republic. Then its members took several months to debate the details of the constitution. For the first time ever, Germany became a democracy – a country ruled by representatives of the people. These representatives would meet in a parliament called the *Reichstag*. As a republic, Germany would also have a president as an elected head of state instead of the Kaiser.

The constitution gave Germans a number of basic rights. These were set out in the 'fundamental laws'.

Source 4.3 — The Fundamental Laws

Personal freedom is guaranteed. No-one can be arrested unless they have broken the law.

The home of every German is a place of safety for him. The authorities cannot enter without proper cause.

Every German has the right to express his opinion freely by word, writing, printed matter or picture.

All Germans have the right to hold peaceful meetings.

All Germans have the right to form unions and societies.

Property is guaranteed.

Activities

1 Copy this paragraph, filling in the blanks:

   The N _____ A _____ was elected in 1919. It met in the city of _____ because it was _____ and less likely to be disturbed by violence than _____. The Assembly had to write a new c _____ for Germany. **(KU)**

2 Why is Source 4.2 valuable as evidence about the new government in Germany in 1919? **(ENQ)**

3 What features of the constitution made Germany a democracy? **(KU)**

4 What rights and protection did the new constitution give to German people? **(KU)**

F/G LEVEL

GENERAL/CREDIT LEVEL

The burden of defeat

Those who met at Weimar knew that it would be hard to make the new republic popular. For one thing, many Germans saw its existence as evidence of national humiliation, as a modern historian has observed in the source below.

Source	4.4	JM Roberts, 'The Age of Upheaval', 1981

In the eyes of many German patriots, the republic was only there because Germany had been defeated and the people who founded it had helped in that defeat. The republic had also signed the peace terms (and would always be blamed for them); it had been born in revolution, and had at once to face the awful practical problems of defeat: the demobilisation of the armies when no jobs were available, the feeding of the cities when the Allied blockade was still kept up.

The Assembly had to reach decisions on difficult issues, including the amount of power that should be given to the new head of state and the method by which the new Parliament (*Reichstag*) should be elected.

These issues caused bitter arguments, as politicians had very different views of what the future Germany should be like.

The work of the assembly

Despite the differences among its members, the Assembly succeeded in agreeing on a constitution. With so many competing ideas, not surprisingly it turned out to be a compromise.

◆ Germany was to have a President as Head of State;

◆ The parliament was to have two parts, the *Reichstag*, elected by the people, and the *Reichsrat*, whose members were nominated by the states (*Länder*);

◆ A Chancellor, chosen by the President from the party leaders in the *Reichstag*, was to be head of the government;

◆ The *Reichstag* proposed new laws but the *Reichsrat* could then debate them and block any supported by less than 2/3rds of the *Reichstag*.

Although now a republic, Germany remained a federal country. This means that power was divided between the national (or federal) government in Berlin and the

Source **4.5** The Main Parties 1919. Some of these were more interested in fighting Communism than making the Republic work

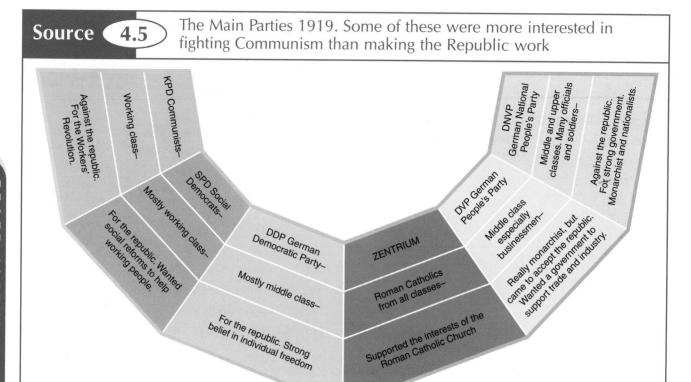

Source **4.6** German People's Party election poster. The caption reads 'Free us from Red chains'

governments of the states (*Länder*) such as Prussia, Bavaria or Saxony. These states had once been separate, but had come together in 1871 to form the German Empire. Many people still identified with their state as much as with Germany. This encouraged the state politicians to want to keep as much power as they could.

Source 4.7 The German states, or *Länder*

Finally, a compromise was reached. The federal government had control of taxation and foreign policy; national laws counted above those of the *Länder*. However, the *Länder* still ran the police, the courts and the schools. By nominating the members of the upper house in the Parliament, the *Reichsrat*, they had an influence over the passing of federal laws.

Two criticisms have often been made of the new arrangement for ruling Germany. First, the President was given special powers.

Source 4.8 Article 48 of the Weimar Constitution 1919

Where public security and order are endangered the President may take the measures necessary for their restoration, intervening if necessary with the help of armed forces. For this purpose he is permitted, for the time being, to set aside the fundamental laws. Such measures shall be withdrawn upon the demand of the Reichstag.

Allowing the President to suspend the constitution and act as a dictator, even temporarily, could be very dangerous.

The second criticism concerned the method of electing the *Reichstag*. The *Reichstag* was to be elected every 4 years by a method called proportional representation. All men and women over the age of 20 were entitled to vote by secret ballot. Parties named lists of candidates in each of the 38 districts, and people voted for the party, not for individual candidates. One name from the list was elected for every 60 000 votes for the party. This system had strengths:

◆ It was a fair system, as each party won seats in the *Reichstag* in proportion to its votes. This meant that all kinds of opinion in Germany would be heard.

◆ No-one had to feel that their vote had been wasted because their candidate was defeated. Every vote helped to elect someone from the party they wanted to support.

It also had weaknesses:

◆ On the other hand, no party was likely to gain a majority in the *Reichstag*, therefore all governments were coalitions, usually involving several parties. Sometimes it could be difficult to keep the partners together for long without disagreeing over policy.

◆ In turn, this meant that it was more difficult to carry through a consistent programme of policies, though it did limit the chance of an extremist government having things all its own way.

Some people have argued that the system of proportional representation was part of the reason for the failure of the Weimar Republic, though a recent German historian has given a different view.

Source **4.9**	Detlev JK Peukert, 'The Weimar Republic', 1993 edn

The results of the 1919 election were not greatly different from the results of the Reichstag election of 1912 in which each constituency had only one member. This continuity in party politics is evidence against the view that proportional representation contributed greatly to the collapse of the Republic. The fact that middle-class parties lost votes in the 1920s was not the result of proportional representation. The rise of the NSDAP [Nazi Party] as a mass party between 1930 and 1932 could not have been blocked by some different form of voting system.

Election by proportional representation did help extremist parties like the Nazis in one way. Even if they could attract only a fairly small number of voters, they were likely to gain a few seats in the *Reichstag*. This meant that Nazi ideas would be heard in the national parliament, and this helped them to grow from a local pressure group into a national party.

By assisting such groups (many of which were dedicated to the overthrow of democracy) to be represented in the *Reichstag*, the new constitution made it more difficult for the Republic to defend itself against its enemies. There were more than enough of these to make democracy very fragile indeed. To many Germans, used to strong leadership under the Kaiser, the whole idea of the Republic seemed weak, and they had little loyalty to it, certainly not enough to defend it when it faced a crisis.

Source **4.10**	**Friedrich Ebert**, the SPD leader who became the first President of the Weimar Republic. Many people see him as the founder of democratic government in Germany

Activities

1 Why was it difficult to write a constitution for Germany in 1919 that would win the approval of most Germans? Look at Sources 4.4, 4.5 and 4.6 to help you find as many reasons as you can. **(KU)**

2 How useful is Source 4.6 as evidence that some German politicians were more interested in fighting Communism than in making the new Republic work? **(ENQ)**

3 Describe the way in which the government of Germany was organised under the new constitution. You should mention the head of state, the organisation of Parliament and the Länder. **(KU)**

4 a) According to Source 4.8, in what circumstances was the President granted special powers? **(KU)**

b) Who was to judge whether these circumstances had occurred? **(KU)**

c) Look at Source 4.8. What might these powers mean for ordinary Germans? (Look back to Source 4.3 to help you.) **(KU)**

d) What safeguard seems to be built in to prevent abuse of these powers? How effective was this likely to be? Explain your answer. **(KU)**

5 Look at Source 4.9. Was proportional representation an important cause of the failure of the Weimar Republic? **(KU)**

Role play

Study the following character sketches of imaginary Germans. Decide which party you think each would have supported in 1919, and what she/he would have thought of the Republic. In your group/class, cast one person in each role, and act out a scene in which they discuss the new republic.

◆ Liesl Vogts – wife of a civil servant. Her son was killed on the Somme in 1916.

◆ Josef Held – sailor who took part in the mutiny in November 1918. He is angry about the murders of Liebknecht and Luxemburg.

◆ Gerda Pfeffer – widow of a carpenter, she is a regular at Mass in the village Roman Catholic Church.

◆ Magda Wentz – a part-time factory worker, who lives in a tenement flat with her parents. Her father is unemployed.

◆ Kurt Adler – a Jewish shopkeeper, who hopes for a fair society in the new Germany.

GENERAL/CREDIT LEVEL

5 The Nazis

The leader

The man who took advantage of the weaknesses of the Republic was not even born in Germany. Adolf Hitler was the son of a civil servant from the small town of Braunau in Austria.

Source 5.1

Hitler as a young politician. Notice the neat suit, collar and tie, slicked back hair, and his expression. Hitler's motto, 'Now I'll show you,' is written in the bottom right

At school, Hitler's record was poor. On leaving, he went to Vienna, hoping to get into the Academy of Fine Arts, but he failed the entrance examination. He scraped a living by taking casual jobs, like colouring picture postcards. In Vienna, he came across many racist ideas, including hatred of the Jews, which became important in Nazi beliefs.

By the time war broke out in 1914, Hitler was living in Munich, in southern Germany. He volunteered at once and fought in France and Belgium. In his dangerous job as a runner, carrying messages between his Company and Headquarters, he was wounded and later gassed. He won the Iron Cross twice and was promoted to corporal.

When the war ended, Hitler was in hospital, recovering from the effects of gas on his eyes. He was horrified at Germany's defeat. He blamed the Jews and politicians, saying they had betrayed the soldiers.

A new party

Back in Munich, Hitler took a job as an army spy. He was sent to report on a group called the German Workers' Party. Soon he saw that he might be able to use this party to put forward his own ideas, so he joined.

Almost at once he found that he had a talent for public speaking.

Source 5.2 — Kurt Ludecke, 'I Knew Hitler', 1938

When the man stepped forward on the platform, there was almost no applause. Then he began to speak, quietly at first. Before long, his voice had risen to a hoarse shriek that gave an extraordinary effect. Leaning [forward] he was holding the masses, and me with them, under a hypnotic spell by the sheer force of his conviction. I do not know how to describe the emotions that swept over me as I heard this man. When he spoke of the disgrace of Germany, I felt ready to spring on any enemy.

He rose quickly to lead the group. On 5 February 1920 he changed its name to the National Socialist German Workers' Party. In German, this gave it the initials NSDAP. From the German spelling of the first work – *Nazional* – this long title was shortened to the Nazi Party.

Source 5.3 — Hitler practising a speech in front of a mirror

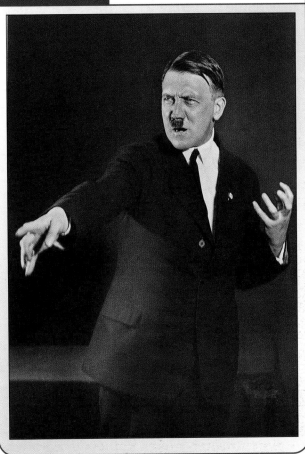

FOUNDATION/GENERAL LEVEL

Activities

1 Why were Hitler's experiences in Vienna and in the war important in forming his ideas? **(KU)**

2 a) Source 5.1 was taken as a publicity photograph. Pick out three things that suggest Hitler wanted to appear respectable. **(ENQ)**

   b) Look as his expression. Choose one word from this list that you think describes it best:
   excited, determined, friendly, sad, angry **(ENQ)**

   c) Why do you think he put on that expression for the camera? **(ENQ)**

3 How can you tell that the writer of Source 5.2 was impressed by Hitler's ability as a speaker? **(ENQ)**

4 In Source 5.3, Hitler is shown in a dramatic pose. Why do you think he used his hands and arms like this in his speeches? **(ENQ)**

The party programme

The foundation of Hitler's new right wing party came at a time when there were many other signs of opposition to the Weimar Republic by extreme nationalist groups. Only a month after their formation there was a *Putsch* – an attempt to seize power – in Berlin led by a civilian called Wolfgang Kapp and supported by some nationalists, rebellious sailors and *Freikorps* members. The army showed its dislike of the Republic by refusing to put down the rebellion, and most of the government had to flee to Stuttgart from Berlin. The revolt was only defeated after the Social Democratic Party (SPD) and the trade union movement called a general strike which showed that the leaders of the revolt had no authority. The revolt collapsed and the leaders fled the country. Further evidence of the strength of nationalist feeling came with a series of political murders. Among those killed were Matthias Erzberger, who had signed the armistice with the Allies in 1918, and the Foreign Minister Walter Rathenau, who was Jewish. It was in this atmosphere that Hitler's party was founded.

From the start, the Nazi party made its policies very clear. Its programme was built around nationalism, racist theories and a belief in strong central government.

Source 5.4	From the Programme of the Nazi party, 1920

- *We demand the union of all Germans in one Great Germany by the right of self-determination of peoples.*

- *We demand land and territory (colonies) for the feeding of our people and for the settlement of our surplus population.*

- *Only those who are members of the nation can be citizens. Only those who are of German blood . . . can be members of the nation. No Jew can, therefore, be a member of the nation.*

- *An understanding of national consciousness must be taught to the children at the earliest possible age.*

- *For the carrying out of all these we demand: the creation of a strong central power in the Reich.*

This programme proved that the Nazis were enemies of democratic government. They were not only opponents of the existing parties; they meant to topple the Weimar Republic itself. Hitler had made his views on democracy plain already. It was weak. It was Jewish. It was *not* German.

The Brownshirts

Like most parties in the 1920s, the Nazis formed their own private army. At first its nature was disguised, but its purpose was not.

> **Source 5.5** Nazi party newspaper, 3 August 1921
>
> *The NSDAP has created its own gymnastic and sports section. It is intended to bind our young party members together. It is intended to provide protection for the propaganda activity of the leaders. But above all it is intended to develop in the hearts of our young supporters a tremendous desire for action, to drive home to them and burn into them the fact that history does not make men, but men history.*

This new force was called the *Sturm Abteilung*, the Storm Section (SA). It was given a uniform with a military-style brown shirt, and trained in army fashion. Its first jobs were to protect Nazi speakers, to prevent opponents from breaking up Nazi meetings, and to disrupt meetings held by other parties. Anxious to project an image of youth and vigour, it was not long before the SA became involved in violence as they tried to drive their enemies, especially the Communists, from the streets.

As early as October 1922, Hitler led 700 SA men, complete with banners and a band, to a 'German Day' parade in the town of Coburg, where they were intercepted by Communists.

> **Source 5.6** SA members in 1923

STOSSTRUPP·HITLER MÜNCHEN

Source **5.7** Kurt Ludecke, 'I Knew Hitler'

We met a great storm of insults from a crowd collected by the Reds to hoot at us. The SA men kept strict formation and ignored the jeers. The turmoil and tension reached a climax when the crowds, incited by agitators, began to throw things and to attack us bodily. Patience could endure no more; now we had to defend ourselves . . .

For nearly quarter of an hour it was an outright battle, man to man. At first the police took no sides, striking at everyone with impartial vigour. But soon, probably because they shared our enthusiastic dislike for the street rabble, most of them took our side, and before long we were master of the field.

This was one of the first of many such clashes in which young Nazis had the chance to prove themselves.

In its early days, the NSDAP was hardly known outside the state of Bavaria. There, in 1923, Hitler saw his first chance to take advantage of the terrible problems ordinary people were facing as the German economy began to collapse.

Source **5.8** Nazi propaganda poster of 1941. The image had not changed since the 1920s. The German caption said 'Service in the SA develops comradeship, toughness, strength'

Activities

1 Why was 1920 a promising time to form a party like the NSDAP? **(KU)**

2 How important was nationalist opposition as a threat to the Weimar Republic in 1921–1922? **(KU)**

3 a) Why is Source 5.4 valuable as evidence that the Nazi party was racist, authoritarian and nationalist? **(ENQ)**

   b) Which of Hitler's youthful experiences influenced the ideas in the Nazis' political programme? Explain your answer. **(KU)**

4 Compare Source 5.4 with Source 4.5 on p. 20. Which other parties would you expect to be i) allies, ii) enemies of the Nazis. Explain your answer. **(ENQ)**

5 How accurate is Source 5.5 as evidence about the reasons for the formation of the SA? **(ENQ)**

6 Look at Source 5.8.

   a) What image of SA members did the artist try to project?

   b) What methods did the artist use to create this image? **(ENQ)**

   c) To what extent do you think the artist succeeded? Explain your answer. **(ENQ)**

Sources 5.6 and 5.7 give evidence about the SA and its activities. Study the sources carefully and answer the questions which follow. You should use your own knowledge where appropriate.

7 Discuss the value of Source 5.6 as evidence of the military character of the SA. **(ENQ)**

8 How far do these sources agree about the part played by the SA in Nazi campaigns? **(ENQ)**

6 Problems in Germany

Inflation

War and blockade had hurt the German economy. The loss of industrial land demanded by the Versailles treaty had made things worse. Now Germany had to pay France and Belgium £100 million a year for 66 years to repair war damage. Most of this had to be paid in goods – coal, iron and timber.

People began to suffer as goods ran short. Prices rose. The government tried to pay its debts by printing more money. This just made prices rise faster, until they were out of control. This is called **inflation**.

Source 6.1

Date	Number of Marks to the Dollar (rounded off)
July 1914	4
July 1920	40
July 1921	80
July 1922	500
January 1923	18 000
July 1923	350 000
September 1923	100 000 000
November 1923	4 000 000 000 000

The face value of banknotes changed nearly every day – hundreds of marks, thousands, millions. By the middle of 1923 they were really worth nothing. People got rid of them for goods, *any* goods. They could always be exchanged for something else later.

Source 6.2
Postage stamps 1921–1923

5 million marks

20 million marks

30 thousand marks

50 million marks

These stamps were overprinted to save printing new ones

20 thousand marks on 200 mark stamp

10 million marks on 50 mark stamp

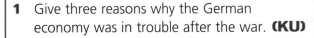

Source 6.3 — A woman remembers life in Berlin, 1923

Two women were going to the bank with a washing basket, filled with notes. They passed a shop and saw a crowd standing round the window, put down the basket for a moment and hurried forward to see if there was anything that could be bought. Then they turned round and found that all the notes were there, untouched. But the basket had gone.

Results

Inflation had a dreadful effect on the standard of living of ordinary Germans. Factories closed and unemployment grew. As the prices of food, clothing and fuel rose, people went cold and hungry. Disease began to spread.

Those who suffered most were the middle classes. The workers had little to lose. Many of the middle classes had been fairly well off. Now they were as poor as the workers. They were ashamed and angry. Of course, they blamed the government.

Activities

1   Give three reasons why the German economy was in trouble after the war. **(KU)**

2   In what ways do Sources 6.1 and 6.2 agree about the value of money in Germany in the years 1921–1923? **(ENQ)**

3   Give two reasons why Source 6.3 is useful evidence about the effects of inflation in Germany in 1923. **(ENQ)**

4   a) What does Source 6.3 tell us about people's attitudes towards money in 1923? **(KU)**

    b) What does Source 6.4 tell us about the effect of inflation on the way in which workers were paid? **(KU)**

5   Why did people in Germany no longer want banknotes by the end of 1923? Use sources 6.1 and 6.3 to help you answer. **(KU)**

Group discussion

Look back at the characters in the role play on p. 23. Which of these people do you think would have been hurt most by the inflation? Explain why you think so.

FOUNDATION/GENERAL LEVEL

Source 6.4 — Wages being taken in washing baskets to workers

Inflation and discontent

By 1921 there was ample cause for discontent in Germany. The final reparations figure stunned everyone. They demanded to know how German agriculture and industry were supposed to produce enough to meet the needs of their own people and the requirements of the Allies as well. Their anger was turned on the politicians of the Weimar Republic. In the 1920 elections, moderate parties lost support to the Nationalists and the Independent Socialists. Political violence continued, with assassinations commonplace.

The Rühr occupation

Early in 1923 German anger was turned outwards. France had complained that Germany had not kept up deliveries of goods due as reparations payments. In February, French and Belgian troops occupied the industrial area of the Rühr to enforce deliveries. German historians have argued that the French also intended the occupation to make permanent the separation of the Rhineland and the Rühr from the rest of Germany.

The German government at once ordered a policy of passive resistance. It told workers, businessmen and officials to refuse to co-operate with the French. It called a general strike, with the government paying the wages of the workers and public servants.

The French reacted by trying to cut off the Rühr from the rest of Germany. They also brought in workers to operate the factories and mines. They arrested many people, and expelled civil servants, police and others. By humiliating people they caused great bitterness.

Source **6.5** 'No! I will not be forced.' A German poster of 1923 urging German miners to refuse to work, even though threatened by French soldiers

Source **6.6** Theodore Abel, then a schoolboy in Wiesbaden

We received rules of conduct at school; but we all knew that none of us would ever salute a French officer. Better hide behind a strange doorway than doff our caps to the enemy.

These policies brought the German people together, supporting the government against the common foe. Their resolution was strengthened when frustration among the occupying troops led to violent clashes resulting in several deaths. Many Germans, especially nationalists, also resented the presence of black soldiers from French African colonies among the forces of occupation. For the moment, national divisions were disguised by hatred of the common enemy.

Inflation out of control

Passive resistance had disastrous economic effects. The government's policy of paying the strikers and compensating those who had suffered financial loss, like the mine owners, could only be carried out by printing more and more paper money. The result was that, very soon, there was too much money in circulation. Prices went up, and the value of the mark collapsed.

In these circumstances, living conditions suffered.

◆ People only ate half as much meat as before the war;

◆ new clothing and soap were almost unobtainable;

◆ basic hygiene in slums was impossible because of over-crowding;

◆ food poisoning increased as people were forced into eating rotten food;

◆ malnutrition was widespread.

It was hard for ordinary people to understand what was happening to them. One person, lucky to find a job, might work all hours for a wage that could not feed and clothe his family. Another, whose savings had seemed security for old age, might find them worth next to nothing. Herr Neisse worked as a gardener in Berlin, saving to get married.

Source 6.7	Christabel Bielenberg, 'The Past is Myself,' 1984

There was no doubt in his mind that the disaster which befell him . . . in 1923 was the result of some dire and treasonable plot. His savings, Hilde's savings, their plot of land, their humble enough hopes, had vanished into thin air overnight . . . "With my savings I was able to buy just one cup and saucer which I gave to Hilde instead of her marriage lines . . ." The loss of his bank account had not only shattered whatever faith he might have had in constitutional government, but also struck at the root of his very being, his self-respect, and his right to be respected.

He was not the only one to lose faith in constitutional government. Bad though the experience was for working-class people, for the middle classes it was many times worse. People who had felt themselves to have a little extra, either in money or status, felt the humiliation of their descent into poverty all the more.

Source **6.8**

Brought down by inflation, middle-class citizens survive by selling their valuables

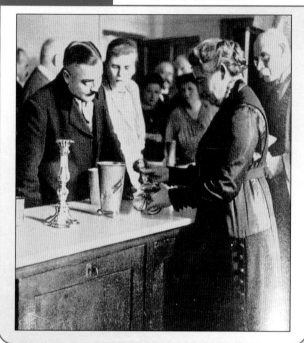

These people's agony gave them a need to blame someone, or something. The someone tended to be those whom they saw as weak politicians; the something to be the Weimar Republic itself. As one historian has observed:

Source **6.9** — **Louis L Snyder**, 'The Weimar Republic,' 1966

Widows, civil servants, teachers, army officers and pensioners lost their lifetime savings. It was the scar that never healed. These were the people who later turned to Adolf Hitler.

Many of these were also the people whose support was critical for the survival of democracy. Their loss of faith threatened to undermine the Republic, as the 1924 election results showed. As for Herr Neisse, in 1931 he joined the Nazi party.

Source **6.10** — Reichstag election results

	1920	1924	
German Democratic Party	44	28	moderate parties
German People's Party	62	44	
Social Democrats	113	100	
Communists	2	62	extremist parties
Nazis	0	32	

Activities

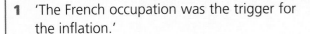

1 'The French occupation was the trigger for the inflation.'

Give a brief account of the reasons for the inflation of 1922–1923. **(KU)**

2 To what extent do Sources 6.5 and 6.6 agree about the German response to the French occupation of the Rühr? **(ENQ)**

3 How accurate is Source 6.7 as evidence of the effects of the inflation on ordinary German people? **(ENQ)**

4 Discuss the value of Source 6.8 as evidence about the impact of the inflation on middle-class Germans? **(ENQ)**

5 'The inflation was the most serious crisis yet for the Weimar Republic.'

Describe fully the effects of the inflation of 1922–1923 on Germany. **(KU)**

Note: for this answer you should write a short essay of several paragraphs.

6 Which of the sources have you found most helpful in understanding inflation in Germany and why? **(ENQ)**

Group discussion

1 Consider these issues as a group. Report back to the class on your conclusions:

a) Give as many reasons as you can why the German people were discontented by 1923. Classify these under the headings:

Political   Economic   Social.

b) Which of these kinds of causes do you think was the most serious? Explain your answer. **(KU)**

2 As a group, make a wallchart to illustrate the crisis of 1923. You might include a graph of the value of the mark, cartoons or pictures, or a poster bringing out the effects of the crisis on ordinary people. **(KU)**

GENERAL/CREDIT LEVEL

7 The Munich Putsch

Hitler's chance

Unlike the northern states like Prussia, the people of Bavaria in southern Germany were mostly Roman Catholics. Many were more loyal to Bavaria than to Germany. This was also a state whose politics were very conservative. Many of the leading politicians did not like socialism. They did not like the fact that the Social Democrats (SPD) were the leading partners in most of the governments in the Weimar Republic. When the inflation came, some of the leaders planned to rise against the government in Berlin.

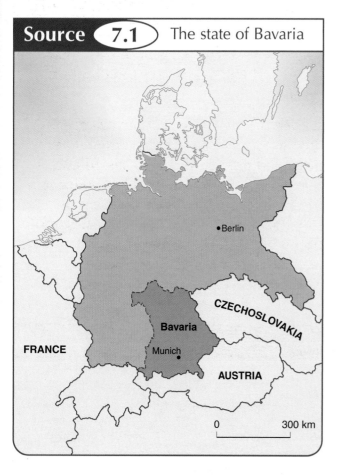

Source 7.1 The state of Bavaria

The Putsch

On 8 November 1923, Herr von Kahr, head of the Bavarian government, spoke at a big meeting in a beer cellar in Munich. General von Lossow (the army Commander in Bavaria) and Colonel von Seisser (the police chief) were with him. Hitler decided to use their meeting to try to seize power.

With some friends, Hitler went into the meeting. He waited until 600 SA men had surrounded the building. When Hermann Göring and 25 of them burst into the hall, Hitler jumped onto a chair and fired a shot into the air. He said that a national revolution had begun.

Hitler forced the three leaders into a side room at gunpoint. They refused to join him, but Hitler went back into the hall and announced that they *had* done. His bluff worked. The crowd cheered him. After General Ludendorff arrived to support Hitler, Kahr, Lossow and Seisser agreed to work with him. Hitler spoke to the crowd about the government in Germany.

Source 7.2 Speech by Hitler, 8 November 1923

The government of the November Criminals is declared to be removed. A new national government will be named this very day in Munich. The task of the National Government is to organise the march on Berlin, and save the German people.

Source 7.3 SA men prepare to advance

Then Hitler made a mistake. He left the beer cellar to sort out a fight between some SA men and ordinary soldiers. At once Lossow and Kahr ordered the army to put down the Nazi rising.

Defeat

While Hitler was at the beer cellar, Nazis took over government buildings.

At the war ministry the army trapped a group headed by the SA leader, **Ernst Röhm**. On the morning of 9 November, Hitler and Ludendorff led a march to the rescue.

As they marched down a narrow street, they were met by the police. Someone fired, and fighting began. It lasted only a minute, but 16 Nazis and three policemen were killed. Hitler was dragged to the ground with a dislocated shoulder. Some friends drove him off in a car, but two days later he was arrested. Hitler and Ludendorff went on trial for treason.

Activities

1 In what two ways were people in Bavaria different from the rest of Germany? **(KU)**

2 Describe how Hitler attempted to seize power in Munich. **(KU)**

3 Explain why his attempt

a) went well at first

b) failed in the end. **(KU)**

4 Give two ways in which Source 7.2 shows that the Nazis opposed the government in Germany. **(ENQ)**

Hitler's trial

Hitler's trial provided a portrait in miniature of the obstacles to the growth of democracy in Germany. It demonstrated clearly the nationalist, conservative bias of the forces of law and order.

Past rebellions by left-wing groups like the Spartacists had been put down ruthlessly. Now the leader of an attempted revolution was allowed by the judges to turn his trial into a publicity stunt. In front of a large number of foreign journalists, Hitler interrupted and insulted the witnesses and made long speeches in which he attacked the Weimar Republic and declared his intention of being a dictator. He made prophecies:

Source **7.4** Hitler speaking at his trial

I believe that the hour will come when the people, who today stand in the street with our swastika banner, will join with those who fired upon them. I believe that this blood will not always separate us. When I learned that it was the police who fired, I was happy that it was not the army. One day the hour will come when the army will stand at our side, officers and men.

He dared the judges to punish him:

Source **7.5** Hitler's closing speech

It is not you, gentlemen, who pass judgement on us. That judgement is spoken by the eternal court of history. That court will judge us as Germans who wanted only the good of their own people and Fatherland; who wanted to fight and die. You may say we are guilty a thousand times over, but the goddess of the eternal court of history will smile and tear to tatters the sentence of this court. For she acquits us.

It was impossible for the court to find Hitler innocent, for he had gloried in his guilt. In contrast to the harsh treatment of left-wing revolutionaries four years previously, Hitler was given the minimum possible sentence of five years' imprisonment. This meant that he might be out on parole after six months. Ludendorff, the old war hero, was released at once.

Source **7.6** Ludendorff and Hitler pose together at the end of the trial

Hitler in Prison

Hitler served his sentence in the fortress of Landsberg, 50 miles west of Munich. His surroundings were pleasant and he and the other Nazis imprisoned with him suffered few restrictions.

Source 7.7 Hitler and his companions in their common room

Source 7.8 Hitler's cell in Landsberg fortress

Source 7.9 Kurt Ludecke describes the routine at Landsberg

Lunch with his fellow-prisoners with Hitler presiding sounded more like a social affair. In the afternoon one prisoner served tea to the others in their cells. Before and after the six o'clock supper . . . they were again free to exercise in the garden for an hour or so.

During the eight months which he actually served in prison, Hitler spent most of the time writing. The result was his book *Mein Kampf* (My Struggle) in which he described his early years and explained his political ideas. He made plain his belief in a revived Germany under a strong leader (himself, of course), his racist ideas and policy of creating a pure 'Aryan' master race by disposing of 'unclean' elements (especially the Jews) and his conviction that Germany must obtain *Lebensraum* (Living Space) for its people by conquest in eastern Europe.

Most people ignored *Mein Kampf*. Its heavy style made it difficult to read, and those who persevered thought it was too wild to be taken seriously as a political statement. They were wrong, as Hitler would prove when he became dictator.

GENERAL/CREDIT LEVEL

Activities

1 Why were Hitler's trial and sentence evidence of democracy's weakness in Germany? **(KU)**

2 What does Source 7.4 show about Hitler's views on
   a) the police?
   b) the army? **(ENQ)**

3 To what extent do Sources 7.5 and 7.6 show that Hitler was proud of his actions? **(ENQ)**

4 Describe Hitler's treatment in prison, as revealed by Sources 7.7, 7.8 and 7.9. **(KU)**

5 What was the importance of 'Mein Kampf' for the future of the Nazi party? **(KU)**

8 Years of Hope 1924–1929

Recovery

Inflation could not be allowed to go on for ever. The outside world could not risk the consequences of complete collapse in Germany. An American banker, **Charles Dawes**, was given the job of preparing a plan to help Germany recover.

With the agreement of the Allies, Dawes arranged for the annual reparations bill to be reduced and for huge American loans to help German industry and trade to regain their strength. The old currency was replaced by the *Rentenmark*, a new mark whose value was guaranteed. The coal and steel industries were modernised. This plan was so successful that by 1927 Germany was producing more goods than in 1913, despite the losses of Versailles. The country began to show at least a few signs of prosperity. This prosperity began to be visible in everyday life.

Source 8.1 A young American journalist recalls life in Germany in 1925

A wonderful spirit was working in Germany. Life seemed more free, more exciting, than any place I had ever seen. And everywhere the accent was on youth. They were a healthy, carefree, sun-worshipping lot and they were filled with an enormous zest for living to the full and in complete freedom.

This new atmosphere in Germany showed itself in other ways. Germany began to share in the optimistic 'Roaring Twenties' atmosphere that affected other countries such as the USA and Britain. For those who could afford it, Berlin became an exciting and lively city, with night clubs, dance halls and all that made up the 'jazz age'. Across the country, new forms of entertainment became popular. The cinema transformed public entertainment; for those who wanted to be entertained at home, by 1929 three million German families owned radio sets.

Germans also took part in modern movements in art, music, literature, science and architecture. Composers like Arnold Schoenberg and Kurt Weill brought new ideas to music, while Bertolt Brecht did the same for the theatre. During the whole period of the Weimar Republic, Albert Einstein was director of the Kaiser Wilhelm Physical Institute in Berlin, where he performed much of the work which won him the Nobel prize for physics in 1921. All of this activity showed a rising confidence in Germany.

International Relations

In other ways too, Germans were regaining their self respect. Under the guidance of the foreign minister, Gustav Stresemann, Germany began to achieve recognition from other powers. In 1925 the Locarno Treaty guaranteed the borders with France and Belgium, and in the following year Germany was invited to join the League of Nations. The Allies also agreed to reduce the forces occupying the Rhineland. Stresemann's personal part in improving international relations was recognised in 1926 when he was awarded the Nobel peace prize.

Source 8.2 The Locarno honeymoon. This photograph shows European leaders and their wives after the signing of the Locarno Treaty in 1925

Results

These advances began to create hope that the Weimar Republic might succeed after all. This was reinforced by the results of the 1928 election, in which the Social Democrats, who were most strongly committed to the Republic, did much better than they had in either of the elections in 1924. The nationalist parties lost ground, but so too did the middle-class parties whose supporters had suffered so much in the inflation. Though the Nazis did badly, a warning that extremists were still dangerous could be seen in the level of support for the Communists. During the 1920s support for the Nazi party came mainly from skilled workers, but also from factory owners and some less skilled workers. Doctors, lawyers and students gave much less support to National Socialism in the 1920s, as did unskilled workers.

Though democratic government was more popular by 1928, its hold on the German people was very fragile. It depended utterly on the economic revival continuing. But the revival itself was very uncertain. It in turn depended too heavily on foreign help, and especially on American loans. If anything were to force the withdrawal of these loans, the results would be disastrous in every sense for Germany. Since his release from prison in December 1924, Adolf Hitler had been preparing carefully to take advantage of any such disaster.

GENERAL/CREDIT LEVEL

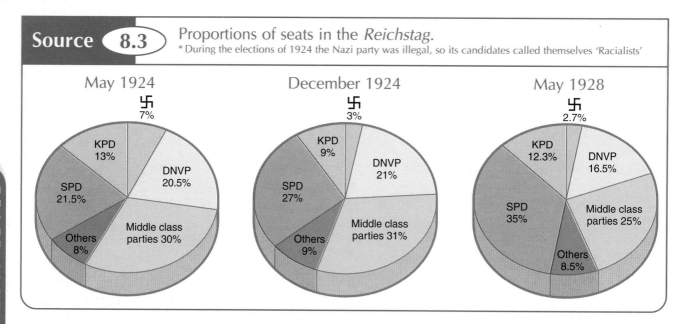

Source **8.3**   Proportions of seats in the *Reichstag*.

*During the elections of 1924 the Nazi party was illegal, so its candidates called themselves 'Racialists'

May 1924

7%
KPD 13%
DNVP 20.5%
SPD 21.5%
Others 8%
Middle class parties 30%

December 1924

3%
KPD 9%
DNVP 21%
SPD 27%
Others 9%
Middle class parties 31%

May 1928

2.7%
KPD 12.3%
DNVP 16.5%
SPD 35%
Middle class parties 25%
Others 8.5%

Activities

1   Why was Germany able to recover from the economic crisis of 1923? **(KU)**

2   What evidence was there that life in Germany was improving in the second half of the 1920s? (Use information from the text and Source 8.1.) **(KU)**

3   How important were events in foreign relations in giving German people more confidence? **(KU)**

4   a)   What signs of hope could be found by comparing the election results of 1924 and 1928? (Source 8.3).

    b)   What warning did the results contain? **(ENQ)**

5   Explain why the Nazi party lost support between 1924 and 1928. **(KU)**

9 Vote for Hitler!

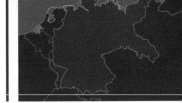

The lessons of failure

In the Munich Putsch, Hitler had tried to seize power using violence. He failed. He decided to give up the idea of revolution. Instead, he would persuade people to vote him into power.

> **Source 9.1** Hitler speaking to a friend in Landsberg prison
>
> *Instead of working to gain power by arms, we shall have to hold our noses and enter the Reichstag against the Catholic and Marxist members. If outvoting them takes longer than outshooting them, at least the results will be guaranteed . . . Sooner or later we shall have a majority, and after that we shall have Germany.*

To get the votes, the party had to be organised. There were to be local branches in as many towns and villages as possible. In this way everyone would hear what the Nazis had to say, and have the chance to vote for them if they wanted.

Winning support

The first thing that Hitler wanted was to give people a good image of the Nazis.

He dressed the SA in smart uniforms. He had them drilled to march behind the swastika flag to the sounds of bands playing stirring and catchy tunes. He gave them colourful banners to march behind. He wanted them to look young, neat,

Source 9.2 Hitler in SA uniform with standard bearer

disciplined and strong. This would attract people to listen to what they had to say.

What the Nazis had to say was simple.

> **Source 9.3** Adolf Hitler 'Mein Kampf'
>
> *The masses* can learn little and understand little. All propaganda must be limited to a few slogans. These slogans should be repeated until the very last person has got hold of the message.*
>
> * masses 5 ordinary people

Here are the main points of the message
that Hitler wanted ordinary people to learn:

The Weimar Republic
is weak

Germany's problems are caused
by Jews and Communists

The German people are
the master race

Adolf Hitler will make
Germany great again

The Nazis trained speakers to deliver this message. They screamed it at public meetings wherever they could gather an audience – in town squares or in village halls. Nazi newspapers carried it in large print. Nazi posters advertised it everywhere. More and more people began to believe it.

Source 9.4

Nazi open air election meeting. Note the lorry loads of stormtroopers. The banner in the bottom right corner means 'Vote List 7' – the Nazi list of candidates in the election

Activities

1 Copy and complete this passage: Hitler's failure at Munich taught him that he would not win power by using _____. Instead, he would try to have Nazis elected to the R _____. He would take power by _____ his enemies. **(KU)**

2 What method did he decide to use to try to gain power in Germany? **(KU)**

3 Read Source 9.1.

   a) What tells you that Hitler did not like the idea of going into the Reichstag? **(ENQ)**

   b) What evidence is there that he knew he would not win quickly? **(ENQ)**

4 In what ways does Source 9.2 support the view that Hitler wanted the Nazis to have a good image? **(ENQ)**

5 Describe three ways in which the Nazis tried to give the SA a good image. **(KU)**

6 What were the main ways Nazis used to deliver their message to ordinary people? **(KU)**

7 a) Is Source 9.4 useful as evidence of the methods used by Nazis during election campaigns? **(ENQ)**

   b) Why do you think stormtroopers attended this meeting? **(KU)**

F/G LEVEL

GENERAL/CREDIT LEVEL

Reorganising the party

At first, the activities of the National Socialist (Nazi) party had been limited mostly to Bavaria. To be a party for the whole nation, its members had to be known throughout Germany. This required a national organisation, which was built up between 1924 and 1929.

Hitler divided Germany up into regions based on *Reichstag* electoral districts. Each was called a Gau and had its own party leader called a *Gauleiter*.

The local branches held meetings and handed out leaflets. Although progress might have been slow, this provided a good framework for action when the opportunity came.

At the same time, Hitler settled a number of quarrels which had threatened to split the party while he was in prison. Quickly he achieved total control over the party, which adopted the *Führerprinzip* (leadership principle) as a key part of its policy.

Propaganda

With the help of **Dr Josef Goebbels**, a publicity expert, Hitler now tried to sell his party to the German people, just as advertisers sell goods. Hitler's instinct told him which approach to favour.

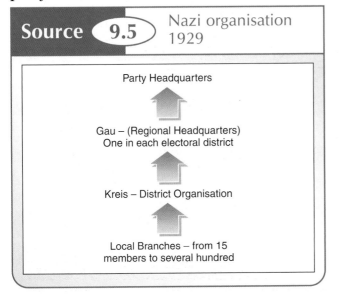

Source 9.5 Nazi organisation 1929

Party Headquarters

↑

Gau – (Regional Headquarters) One in each electoral district

↑

Kreis – District Organisation

↑

Local Branches – from 15 members to several hundred

GENERAL/CREDIT LEVEL

Source 9.6 — ZAB Zeman, 'Nazi Propaganda', 1973

He knew that a politically uneducated mass public was bound to react to emotion rather than to rational argument. Propaganda had to concentrate on as few points as possible, it had to hammer them home repeatedly, it had to present them in terms of black and white. It could make no concessions to the other side.

He also knew that the most powerful method of influencing people was by speaking to them directly. This was convenient, for his greatest talent was oratory.

Hitler took advantage of this gift by addressing as many public meetings as possible. In order to make the greatest impact, he planned his delivery to the last word and the last gesture, rehearsing in front of a mirror (see Source 5.3, p. 25). Frequently, he would arrive late, so that the tension in the audience mounted. His entry, heralded by military music and escorted by SA men in uniform waving banners, was as dramatic as possible. When he began speaking to a hushed audience, his speech was often slow and halting at first, as though he was unsure of himself. Then, gradually, his pace and volume would increase until he was screaming his slogans, his audience now worked into a frenzy of excitement.

As well as Hitler, the Nazis trained other speakers to travel the country and spread the Nazi message. These talks concentrated on local issues. Often the politics followed an event of some sort.

Source 9.7 — William Carr, 'A History of Germany 1915–1945,' 1979

His rasping voice rarely failed to have an uncanny hypnotic effect on the audience. He never reasoned with audiences but simply put into words what they were longing to hear, feeding on their hidden anxieties and forcing his listeners to surrender their will to that of the leader.

Source 9.8 — Report, Prussian Ministry of the Interior, May 1930

Frequently such propaganda squads stay in a certain place for several days and try to win the population for the movement through the most varied sorts of entertainment such as concerts, sports days and even church parades.

Other parades were central to the Nazi campaign. The smart uniforms of the SA were highly visible on the streets.

The Brownshirts had several functions. They helped to provide the party with a youthful, virile, disciplined image in the military tradition so familiar to Germans.

Source 9.9 — SA Order number 3, November 1926

The SA will appear in public only in closed formation. The sight of a large number of men inwardly and outwardly disciplined, whose total commitment to fighting is clear or can be sensed, makes the deepest impression on every German.

Source 9.10 SA parade in Kreuzberg

They were also used to spice the propaganda campaign with a dash of intimidation. They broke up opponents' meetings and protected their own, and picked street fights at favourable odds with enemy private armies, especially the Communists' *Rotfront* (Red Front). By giving people nightmares on the one hand, and promising them their dreams on the other, the Nazis hoped to build support.

Source 9.11 A Nazi rally in Frankfurt in 1932

Source 9.12

Nazi poster, 'National Race for SA'. On the left, young people salute the troops; in the middle a priest raises his hands in prayer; on the right a capitalist grasps at the SA man's leg

The Nazis exploited the mass media. The *Völkischer Beobachter*, which they bought in Munich in 1920, was only the first of many Nazi newspapers published throughout Germany. The real publicity breakthrough came in 1929, when Hitler was fortunate enough to impress the leader of the Nationalist Party (DNVP), Alfred Hugenberg, who owned a chain of cinemas. The two men agreed to co-operate in a campaign against a new plan to amend reparations payments, the Young Plan. Although the campaign failed, Nazi meetings were featured in newsreels in Hugenberg's cinemas. It was wonderful publicity, letting people all over Germany see on the screen the marching bands, the banners, the uniforms of the SA, so drawing the movement to the attention of Germans who might hardly have been aware of it previously.

The Nazis used modern technology even more spectacularly with the 'Hitler over Germany' campaign during the 1932 Presidential election, when Hitler visited 21 towns in 6 days.

Source 9.13

Dr Josef Goebbels' diary, 18 March 1932

A critical innovation: the Leader will conduct his next campaign by 'plane. By this means he will be able to speak three or four times a day at various places and address about one and a half million people in spite of the time being so short.

During that campaign Goebbels ordered triple the usual number of copies of party newspapers to be printed, with two-thirds of them being distributed free.

Methods of publicity

Apart from the spoken word, the Nazis used a variety of methods to gain public attention. Even the rallies and marches had a visual side, with Nazi symbols shown off proudly.

Visual propaganda was not limited to the display of symbols. Nazi slogans appeared on walls, and the party made widespread use of posters to put across their ideas.

Something for everyone

In its early years the movement tried to win

Source 9.14: Propaganda posters from the 1932 election campaign. The posters on the left promise freedom for children and those on the right promise work and bread

working-class support in the cities. Progress was slow, for most remained loyal to the working-class parties – the Social Democrats (SPD) and Communists (KPD). Even in the election of July 1932, when the Nazis had their biggest success at the polls, their support was 10% lower in cities with over 100 000 inhabitants than in Germany as a whole. This was partly because it was in the cities that the SPD and the KPD organisations were strongest and the loyalty of their supporters hardest to break down.

Source 9.15 Dick Geary, 'Who Voted for the Nazis?', 'History Today', October 1998

Voters in large urban centres were less susceptible to Nazi propaganda. Though there had been a significant increase in support among German workers between 1930 and 1932, this was less marked in the larger cities. Nearly half the working-class newcomers to the party ranks between 1925 and 1932 came from villages of under 5000 inhabitants.

From about 1927, the Nazis took their attention away from the cities. They noticed that farmers were suffering from low prices for their produce, so they developed new policies aimed at the countryside and small towns. They blamed the banks and, of course, the Jews for the farmers' troubles, and promised them lower taxes and rents. They also found out that meetings were more successful in smaller centres.

| Source **9.16** | 'Völkischer Beobachter', 31 May 1928 |

In small towns and villages mass meetings with good speakers are events and are often talked about for weeks, while in big cities the effects of meetings with even three or four thousand people soon disappear.

By 1930 13.2 per cent of party members were farmers.

The Nazis also turned their propaganda on the middle classes (*Mittelstand*), especially the self-employed who had been among those to suffer most from the inflation in 1923. Special leaflets highlighted the problems of small businessmen, craftsmen and shopkeepers. They told these people they were being exploited for the benefit of the Weimar politicians. Here, too, the Nazis were successful, for in the elections of 1930 and 1932 it was the middle-class parties which lost most support to the Nazis.

Activities

1 Explain fully the ways in which the NSDAP publicised its views throughout Germany. **(KU)**

2 How far does the evidence in Source 9.3 support the views of the historian in Source 9.6? **(ENQ)**

3 a) How accurate is Source 9.7 as a judgement on Hitler's effectiveness as a speaker? **(ENQ)**

   b) What evidence in Source 5.2 (p. 25) supports the views of Carr in Source 9.7? **(ENQ)**

4 How important a part did the SA play in Nazi propaganda? Look at Sources 9.4, 9.9 and 9.10 for evidence. **(KU)**

5 Describe the methods used by the Nazis to try to reach as many people as possible with their message. Look at Sources 9.8, 9.11, 9.13 and 9.14 for evidence. **(KU)**

6 'The Nazi propaganda campaign was very important in gaining support for the party.' How far do you agree with this statement? **(KU)**

   Note: for this answer you should write a short essay of several paragraphs.

10 The Nazis Come to Power

Depression

In October 1929 the value of shares on the **American Stock Exchange** suddenly collapsed. Many of the people who owned them lost fortunes. This was also true of banks, which had millions of dollars in shares.

These banks had lent money to factory owners, shopkeepers, traders and other business people. Now they asked them to repay the money. Many could not, and had to close down.

The Americans had lent money to other countries as well, including Germany. These countries, too, had to pay back their loans. As a result, there was less trade, factories closed, and unemployment grew. In this depression, Germany suffered dreadfully.

Source 10.2 — Alan Bullock, 'Hitler: A Study in Tyranny', 1962

Think of these figures in terms of men standing helplessly on the street corners of every industrial town in Germany; of houses without food and warmth; of boys and girls leaving school without any chance of a job, and one may begin to guess something of the anxiety and bitterness burned into the minds of ordinary German working men and women.

The coalition governments of the Republic seemed unable to solve the problem. The parties which formed them began to fall out. First one government resigned, then another. People started to lose what faith they had left in the system.

Source 10.1 — Unemployment in Germany

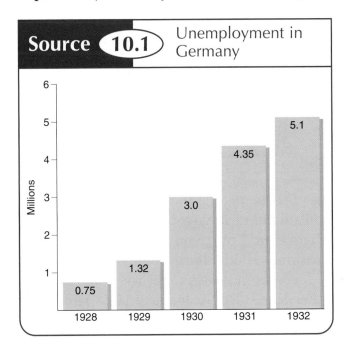

Source 10.3 — Unemployed men on a street corner in Hanover

More and more people were willing to listen to those who claimed to have a simple solution for Germany's troubles. Extremist parties gained more and more support. Some turned to the Communists and joined the Red Front (*Rotfront*); others were happy to hear Hitler's promises. There was increasing violence on the streets as private armies fought each other.

Others saw how popular they were, and hoped to use them for their own purposes: the Nationalists thought they could share power with Hitler; industrialists thought the Nazis would defend them against trade unions and Communists, so they gave Hitler money; army officers thought the Nazis would give the army back its important place in Germany.

Source 10.4

Nazi poster. The German words say 'Our last hope. Hitler.'

Source 10.5

Magazine cover 1932. The German words say: 'The meaning of the Hitler salute. Millions stand behind me. Little man asks for great gifts.'

Mistakes

Nazi support showed in elections. In 1928 less than a million people voted for them, but in 1930 they had nearly 6.5 million votes and in July 1932 over 13.5 million. By then, they were the largest party in the *Reichstag*, though they could not form a government alone.

All of these people thought they could control Hitler in government. A former Chancellor, Franz von Papen, persuaded President Hindenburg to make Hitler leader of a coalition government with only two other Nazis. On 30 January 1933 Hitler became Chancellor of Germany.

Activities

1 What two economic problems faced Germany at the end of 1929? **(KU)**

2 Give three political results of Germany's economic difficulties in 1929. **(KU)**

3 Compare the views of unemployment in

Germany shown in Sources 10.2 and 10.3. **(ENQ)**

4 Why do you think Hitler became Chancellor of Germany in 1933? Give three reasons. **(KU)**

The Nazi revolution
The *Reichstag* fire

Hitler was Chancellor, but he did not yet have full power. Only two other Nazis were in the government. Even with support from the Nationalists, he did not have a majority in the *Reichstag*. Hitler called an election for March 1933, hoping to win enough seats to run Germany as he liked.

One week before the election, Hitler was having dinner with Goebbels and some other Nazis when dramatic news reached him.

Source **10.6**	Dr Josef Goebbels' **diary**, 27 February 1933

Suddenly a 'phone call from Dr Hanfstaengl: 'The Reichstag is on Fire!' I think this is a piece of wild fantasy and refuse to report it to the Leader (Führer). I ask for news wherever possible and at last obtain the dreadful confirmation: it is true! I immediately inform the Führer and we hasten at top speed to the Reichstag. The whole building is aflame. There is no doubt that Communism has made a last attempt to cause disorder by means of fear and terror, in order to grasp power during the general panic.

A young Dutchman called Marinus van der Lubbe was found in the building. He had taken off his shirt and set it alight. Then he had run through the building using it to set fire to old furniture and curtains.

Source **10.7**	The *Reichstag* building on fire. Only some parts of the building were damaged badly

DEM DEUTSCHEN VOLKE

His claim to be a Communist was all Hitler needed as an excuse to act. Out of control with excitement, he yelled,

Source 10.8 — Hitler's orders given at the burning *Reichstag*

Every Communist official must be shot. All Communist deputies must be hanged this very night. All friends of the Communists must be locked up.

At once Hitler asked President Hindenburg for special powers. He got them. The fundamental laws in the Weimar Constitution (see Chapter 4) were suspended. Many Communists were arrested, as the Nazis claimed they had planned a revolution. Hitler hoped that fear of Communism would make many Germans vote for his party in the elections.

As for poor van der Lubbe, although even the police chief thought he was crazy, he was tried and executed.

Source 10.9 — Photograph of van der Lubbe, taken at his trial

Activities

1 Why did Hitler want another election in March 1933? Give two reasons. **(KU)**

2 Why was the Reichstag fire useful to Hitler? **(KU)**

3 Was the writer of Source 10.6 taken by surprise by news of the fire? **(ENQ)**

4 Give two reasons why Source 10.6 is useful evidence about Nazi attitudes towards Communists. **(ENQ)**

5 Look at Source 10.8. What was Hitler's reaction to the fire? **(ENQ)**

Imaginative reconstruction

Using the information in the text and sources, write a report on the fire as though you were reporting it for a radio news programme. You should describe what has happened, comment on the reaction of people who are present, and say what you think will happen next.

Role play

The class should divide into groups, representing political parties as follows: Communist Party (KPD), Social Democratic Party (SPD), Centre Party (ZENTRUM), German National People's Party (DNVP), National Socialist German Workers' Party (NSDAP).

Preparation

In your group, use the information you have learned in the course so far to make up two lists:

◆ arguments in favour of your own party, explaining its main ideas and strengths.

GENERAL/CREDIT LEVEL

Activities continued

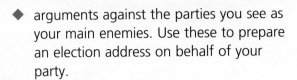

◆ arguments against the parties you see as your main enemies. Use these to prepare an election address on behalf of your party.

The meeting

One person from each group reads the party's election address to the class. There is then a question session, when members of each group can challenge the others on points made in their speeches.

If you wish, a vote can then be taken. In this vote, groups may not vote for their own party.

Terror against the reds

Almost as soon as news of the *Reichstag* fire spread, there were stories that the Nazis had started it themselves. Many of their opponents believed that members of the SA had begun the fire in order to give the Nazis an excuse to attack their enemies. The fire seemed just too convenient for them, especially with van der Lubbe's claim to be a member of the Dutch Communist Party. The German Communist party (KPD) at once made enquiries in Holland.

Source 10.10 Special editions of Communist newspaper, 28 February 1933

We immediately telegraphed our sister party in Holland, and we can confirm that the accused is completely unknown, and has never belonged to the Communist Party.

Most historians now accept that the fire was, in fact, the work of van der Lubbe, acting on his own. The speed of the Nazis in exploiting the opportunity was remarkable, however. The day after the fire President Hindenburg issued a decree under Article 48 of the Constitution (see Source 4.8, p. 21).

Source 10.11 Decree for the Protection of the People and State, 28 February 1933

Restrictions on personal liberty, on the right of free expression of opinion, including freedom of the press, on the right of assembly and violations on the privacy of postal and telephone communications, are allowed beyond the legal limits otherwise set out.

The Nazis did not even wait for the decree. During the night they used the SA as extra police to drag known Communists from their homes, and raided Karl Liebknecht House, the Communist Party headquarters. Nearly 5000 people were arrested.

To justify their actions, the government announced that their raid on Karl Liebknecht House had uncovered plans for a Communist campaign of terror including arson attacks, the kidnapping of families of police officers for use as human shields, and torture of opponents. In reply, the Communists claimed the entire exercise was prepared in advance against themselves and the whole working class. Such actions were designed to make Nazi success in the elections more certain.

Source **10.12** SA man acting as auxiliary policeman guards Communist prisoners

The March election

In the last week before the election, the Nazis were in evidence everywhere. Parades, demonstrations, flags and loudspeakers spread their message, while the SA intimidated their opponents and tore down their posters, replacing them with Nazi ones. Hitler was clever enough not to outlaw the Communist Party (KPD) yet, so that the workers' votes would be divided between them and the Social Democrats (SPD). In this way, fewer Social Democrats would be elected and their strength as opponents in the *Reichstag* would be reduced.

With all this pressure, the election result was amazing. The Nazis did increase their vote enough to become the largest single party with 288 seats, but they did not gain a majority – 56 per cent of Germans voted against them.

Source **10.13** *Reichstag* election results – March 1933

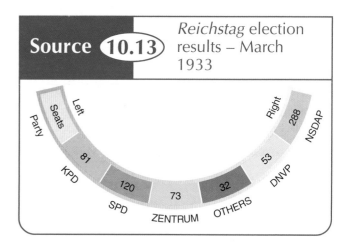

The enabling law

The members of the *Reichstag* met in Berlin's Kroll Opera House on 23 March. The Nazis had set the scene to make the greatest impact possible. A huge swastika banner covered the wall behind the government seats. The National Socialist deputies, dressed in SA uniforms, welcomed Hitler with arms outstretched in salute. The deputies from the other parties had to pass through lines of SS men outside the building and SA men in every corridor. The atmosphere was intimidating.

The results of the election had not given Hitler the majority which would give him complete control of the *Reichstag* and allow him to carry out Nazi policies. He demanded that the *Reichstag* pass an Enabling Law which would give him this power. Under the Constitution, Hitler needed a two-thirds majority to pass the law. Partly from fear, and partly because Hitler promised to respect the rights of the Roman Catholic Church, the mainly Catholic Zentrum Party voted for the law. As the Communist deputies were not even allowed inside the hall, this vote was decisive. When the vote was taken, only 94 brave Social Democrats voted against.

Source **10.14**	Enabling Law, 24 March 1933
Article 1.	In addition to the procedure for passing laws outlined in the Constitution, the Reich Cabinet is authorised to make laws . . .
Article 2.	The laws enacted by the Reich Cabinet may deviate from the Constitution . . .
Article 3.	The national laws enacted by the Reich Cabinet shall be prepared by the Chancellor and published . . .

When **Hermann Göering** announced the result, the Nazis rose as one to roar their approval. Giving the Nazi salute, they sang the Horst Wessel song, their party's theme tune. Their triumph was echoed by cheering crowds outside.

Source **10.15**	Alan Bullock, 'Hitler: A Study in Tyranny', 1962 edition
The street gangs had seized control of the resources of a modern state, the gutter had come to power.	

In effect, the Enabling Law freed Hitler to do as he pleased. Not only did he no longer have to consult the *Reichstag*, he did not even have to refer to the President before acting. He could ignore the Constitution completely.

Other political parties gradually vanished. The KPD had been dealt with already. In June the government banned the SPD. With no real parliament, the Democrats, Nationalists and Zentrum found that they had no purpose left, so dissolved themselves. In July a new law stated that the Nazi Party was the only legal party in Germany. It became a criminal offence to form another party. In only six months, the Nazis had destroyed all trace of democratic government in Germany.

What allowed Hitler to come to power

Ever since 1933 people have asked why it was possible for vicious thugs like the Nazis to come to power in a country with the traditions of Germany. Some think the causes go back to 1918 and the foundation of the Weimar Republic itself, which had a democratic constitution many Germans saw as weak. Others believe these issues could have been resolved but for the experience of mass unemployment during the depression 1929–1932. Some believe the strength, determination, images and propaganda of the Nazi movement explain its success. Yet others argue that all of these factors could have been overcome but for the attitude of some groups within Germany – for example, big business, the civil service, Nationalist politicians and the army.

Activities

1 a) Why do you think that the German Communists sent a telegram (Source 10.10) to the Dutch Communists?

b) Why would they have been so anxious to show that van der Lubbe was not a genuine Communist? **(KU)**

2 Compare the evidence about ways in which the Nazis used the *Reichstag* fire to act against their opponents in Sources 10.11 and 10.12. **(ENQ)**

3 What were the most important results of the *Reichstag* fire? **(KU)**

4 How useful is the Enabling Law (Source 10.14) as evidence of the Nazis' attitude towards democracy? **(ENQ)**

5 Did the Enabling Law mark the end of democracy in Germany? **(KU)**

6 Why do you think the Nazi party was able to take control of Germany in 1933? **(KU)**

GENERAL/CREDIT LEVEL

11 <u>Der Führer</u>

Dictatorship

On 2 August 1934 President Hindenburg died. At once, Adolf Hitler became President as well as Chancellor. He was to be known as *Der Führer* – the Leader. He was also Commander-in-Chief of the Armed Forces. At last he had complete power in Germany.

Governments treat their people in different ways. Some are fair and kind, but others are harsh and cruel. The way they work depends on what they want to do.

The men who started the Weimar Republic wanted all Germans to have a say in government. They gave each adult person a vote. They wanted Germans to be free, so they gave each person rights. (You will find them in Source 4.3, p. 18.)

Hitler's Nazis wanted to keep power for themselves. The SA and the new secret police, the Gestapo, arrested people who might oppose the government. They were sent to the first **concentration camps** in Germany.

It was dangerous to speak against the Nazis, even in private. Spies were everywhere. People were encouraged to report friends, neighbours, even relations who said the wrong thing. When one person vanished during the night it was easier for others to keep quiet.

Source **11.1** Communists are arrested in Chemnitz, 1933

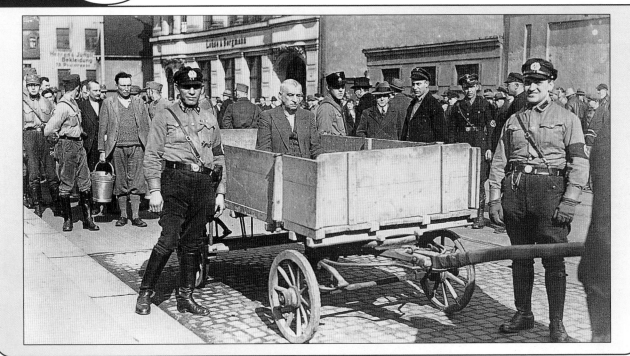

FOUNDATION/GENERAL LEVEL

To strengthen Germany, the Nazis said that they wanted to create a 'pure' German people – a 'master race', the *Herrenvolk*. This meant getting rid of everyone who did not match their standards. Cripples and the mentally ill were not seen as fit enough for the new Germany. The Nazis put many of them in hospitals and nursing homes, but instead of being treated they were killed. Their families were told that they had died from disease.

Other people were not seen as real Germans. Those who came from eastern Europe, black people and especially the Jews were regarded as unfit to be Germans. People like these suffered dreadfully under the Nazis.

The leader

Hitler's government was cruel. It hurt or frightened many Germans. Yet Hitler himself was very popular. He tried to appear as someone who really cared for his people. He made sure that he was photographed among them as often as possible – with members of Nazi organisations, with children, with the workers.

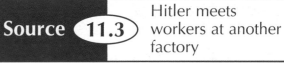

Source 11.3 — Hitler meets workers at another factory

Even when people dared to complain about Nazi rule, they blamed his followers, not Hitler himself. 'If the *Führer* knew about it . . .', they would say, believing he would sort out the problems.

Source 11.4 — A specially posed propaganda shot of Hitler. Note the admiration on the faces of the young people

Source 11.2 — Hitler visits a factory in 1935. A common caption was, 'Bond with the workers'

Activities

1 Describe three ways in which the Nazis treated their opponents. **(KU)**

2 What reason did the Nazis give for treating some people badly? **(KU)**

3 Why did Hitler remain popular with most Germans? **(KU)**

4 In what ways do Sources 11.2 and 11.3 try to make you think well of Hitler? **(ENQ)**

5 How accurate is Source 11.4 as evidence about Hitler's popularity with young people in Germany? You should use your own knowledge and give reasons for your answer. **(ENQ)**

Hitler's government

In Hitler's first months in power the only other Nazis in his Cabinet were Wilhelm Frick, as Minister of the Interior, and Hermann Göring, whose main responsibilities were in the **Prussian** state government. The Nationalists and other conservatives who shared power with the Nazis expected to control them. They were taken aback at the pace at which the Nazis moved.

Göring's position let him replace many senior civil servants, including police officers, with Nazis. He issued orders to the police to oppose socialist or communist organisations, but to support nationalist groups. He even enlisted 40 000 SA and SS men as auxiliary policemen. This made it easy to squash their opponents after the *Reichstag* fire.

By the end of June 1933 the other members of the coalition, except for Vice-Chancellor von Papen, had been replaced by Nazis. With the elimination of other parties by July, it seemed that the Nazi seizure of power was complete.

The night of the long knives

Hitler's main problem now lay within the party. Having helped him to reach power, Ernst Röhm's SA was now a liability. Röhm wanted his SA to become the core of a new German army into which the existing army would be absorbed. More importantly, he demanded that the revolution should not end, but change direction.

> **Source 11.5** Ernst Röhm, July 1933
>
> *Anyone who wanted to be a fellow traveller only during shining torchlight processions and impressive parades and now believes that he has taken part in the German revolution can go home! He has confused the 'national uprising' with the German revolution! If bourgeois simpletons think it is enough that the State has received a new sign, that the 'national' revolution has already lasted too long, for once we agree with them. It is in fact high time the national revolution stopped and became the National Socialist one. Whether they like it or not, we will continue our struggle – if they understand at last what it is about – with them; if they are unwilling – without them; and if necessary – against them*

GENERAL/CREDIT LEVEL

This kind of talk worried Hitler. He needed a period of stability to gain the confidence of the army, the civil service and German business. If they feared a social revolution they could still act together to overthrow him.

Röhm's enemies in the NSDAP, led by Göring and SS leader Heinrich Himmler, persuaded Hitler that Röhm was planning to use the SA to seize power himself. The *Führer* decided to act.

On 30 June 1934 Hitler went to Wiessee, a resort in Bavaria, where the SA leaders were meeting. Supported by **SS** men, he arrested Röhm personally while others rounded up the remaining SA officers. They were taken to Stadelheim Prison in Munich. Two SS men were taken to Röhm's cell.

Source 11.6   Account by the prison governor

There they handed a Browning to Röhm, who asked to speak to Hitler. They ordered him to shoot himself. If he did not comply, they would come back in ten minutes and kill him. When the time was up, the two SS men re-entered the cell, and found Röhm standing with his chest bared. Immediately one of them from the door shot him in the throat.

In Berlin, Munich and other cities, SA leaders were murdered along with others who had incurred Nazi anger. In total, over 400 people were killed, including former Nazi leader Gregor Strasser, army General Schleicher and the retired Bavarian leader, von Kahr.

Source 11.7   A contemporary cartoon from Czechoslovakia

THEY SALUTE WITH BOTH HANDS NOW.

Two weeks later, Hitler spoke to the *Reichstag*. After accusing the SA leaders of corruption and revolutionary ambition, he defended his own actions.

The message to other possible opponents was clear.

Source 11.9 Hitler's speech, 13 July 1934

If anyone asks why I did not resort to the regular courts of justice, then all I can say to him is this: in this hour I was responsible for the fate of the German people, and thereby I became the supreme judge of the German people. I gave the order to shoot the ringleaders in this treason.

GENERAL/CREDIT LEVEL

Activities

1   Using the information in Chapters 10 and 11, make a list of the reasons why the Nazis were able to take complete control of Germany so quickly in 1933. Which of these do you regard as the most important reason? Explain your answer. **(KU)**

2   Why did the SA appear to be a possible threat to Hitler's power by 1934? **(KU)**

3   a)   What evidence in Source 11.5 shows that Röhm did not think the Nazis had achieved all of their aims by gaining power? **(ENQ)**

   b)   How valuable is Source 11.5 as evidence that Röhm presented a threat to Hitler? **(ENQ)**

4   a)   Describe how Hitler rid himself of the danger to his rule presented by the SA. **(KU)**

   b)   What justification for his actions did he give in Source 11.9? **(KU)**

5   Compare the views of Hitler and his actions in Sources 11.7 and 11.8. Explain in detail how each artist has created the impression he wanted. **(ENQ)**

6   Which of these interpretations do you think is the more accurate? Give reasons for your answer. **(ENQ)**

Co-ordination

Nazi rule meant the close supervision of all aspects of life. Germans were encouraged to adopt a Nazi outlook. Those who would not be encouraged were terrorised into doing so, at least in public.

The party had representatives everywhere, from the block wardens who watched the inhabitants of a street to the **SS** men used as labour police on the factory floor.

Source 11.10 Letter from a German worker, January 1939

The lives of us all are continually threatened, and we are under observation all the time. They keep a record of every one of us on a card index, and on it they write whether we give anything for the Winter Help*, whether we put out flags, how big the flags are, and how we hang them. I have never occupied myself with politics but suddenly everything has become political, whatever I say or do, or whatever I don't say or don't do.

*Winter Help was a fund that was supposed to give relief to the poor, but was often used for party purposes.

Hitler was very clear about his purpose. In 1933 he told a meeting of generals that the public had to learn to think as a nation, so that Germany's strength could be restored. This helps to explain the censorship which tried to destroy anything that did not fit into the Nazi version of German nationality.

The nation was to be welded together by a process of 'Co-ordination' (*Gleichschaltung* – the literal meaning is 'putting into the same gear'). Opponents had to be silenced while organisations from the churches to sports clubs had to take on a suitably German identity.

The Nazis regarded Trade Unions as dangerous because they might give the workers an alternative loyalty. They were made illegal, their leaders were jailed and they were replaced by the Labour Front (*Arbeitsfront*). Under the leadership of Robert Ley, it pretended to represent the workers, but its real function was to give

GENERAL/CREDIT LEVEL

Source 11.11 SA men collect 'un-German' books for burning

Germany a disciplined work-force. Other possible centres of opposition suffered too. Within a year, half of the teaching staff at Düsseldorf University and a third of those in Berlin and Frankfurt had been dismissed.

Concentration camps

The concentration camps were not reserved for the Jews. Anyone who was inconvenient for the Nazis – politicians, union leaders, the mentally ill or physically crippled – could be sent there. These camps were run according to tough rules.

Source 11.12 From the rules of Lichtenburg concentration camp

Reporting sick without reason – penalty, 5 days of confinement to cells and several weeks of hard labour.

Making disrespectful remarks about an SS man or deliberately failing to salute – penalty, 8 days' confinement to cells, 25 strokes of the birch at the beginning of the period and another 25 at the end.

Talking politics, making speeches, collecting true or untrue information about the concentration camps – penalty, those committing these offences will be hanged.

Many millions of people suffered terribly in the camps. Their hair was shaved off and they were forced to wear prison uniforms. They had to work very hard, with very little food. At Buchenwald alone, over 33 000 people died in eight years, one in every seven of those who were sent there.

The cruelty of the camps and the air of menace brought about by the sudden arrests and the constant presence of the SS and Gestapo frightened many ordinary Germans into accepting Nazi rule, or at least being unwilling to oppose it openly.

Source 11.13

'As in the Middle Ages, so in the Third Reich.' In this photomontage the artist John Heartfield shows the swastika as a modern weapon of torture like the medieval wheel

Source 11.14

WIE IM MITTELALTER ...

... SO IM DRITTEN REICH

Prisoners at Oranienburg concentration camp working as part of a construction team 1938

Activities

1. a) What evidence in Source 11.10 shows that ordinary Germans believed they were being watched constantly? **(ENQ)**

   b) Think of the practical problems in gathering and using such information. How justified do you think the views expressed in Source 11.10 were? **(ENQ)**

   c) Even if these beliefs were exaggerated, what does this source tell you about life in Nazi Germany? **(KU)**

2. How important was the policy of 'Co-ordination' (*Gleichschaltung*) in establishing Nazi control over everyday life in Germany? **(KU)**

3. How accurate is Source 11.14 as a view of Nazi rule in Germany? **(ENQ)**

4. 'The Nazis were determined to extend their rule over every aspect of German life.'

   Give a brief account of the methods used by the Nazis to control people's lives in Germany.

   Note: For this answer you should write a short essay of several paragraphs. **(KU)**

12 'The Master Race'

The Jews

When Hitler was a boy many people in Germany and other countries disliked the Jews. This hatred of Jews is called anti-Semitism. It happened for several reasons.

They had a different religion from most people in Germany.

Some Jews wore special clothes. This made them easy to pick out.

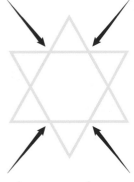

In some cities Jews lived close together. They seemed to be a separate community.

Jews were often very successful in business. This made some Germans jealous.

Hitler first became aware of Jews while in Vienna.

Source 12.1 — **Adolf Hitler**, 'Mein Kampf'

One day, when passing through the Inner City of Vienna, I suddenly saw a creature in a long caftan [robe]. My first thought was: is this a Jew? I watched the man secretly, but the longer I gazed, the more the question shaped in my brain: is this a German?

Source 12.2

Poster for a film called 'The Eternal Jew', 1937. The hammer and sickle of Communism are on a map of Germany, and the coins suggest money lending. The drawing of the Jew is a caricature of what the Nazis said Jews looked like

The Nazis blamed the Jews for Germany's problems after the war. They said that the Jews were Communists and that Jewish greed was ruining the German economy. These two statements did not make sense. If one were true, the other had to be false.

Source 12.3 SA men support a boycott of Jewish shops in April 1933

This did not bother the Nazis. They intended only to give the German people a target for their anger.

Cruelty

Once in power, the Nazis acted against the Jews. Jewish doctors, lawyers and civil servants were sacked. Germans were urged not to use Jewish shops.

Teachers and pupils made fun of Jewish children in schools. Some were ordered to the front of their classes and humiliated by comments about their appearance and way of life. They were told that they were not really Germans. Some children were victims of violent attacks. Many Jews were arrested and sent to concentration camps, at first to be used as slave labour.

If things were not bad enough, in 1938 a young Jew murdered a German official in Paris. This was used as an excuse for 'Kristallnacht', the 'night of broken glass'. All across Germany there were attacks on Jews and their property, many of them begun by the SA. Hundreds of houses and shops were destroyed and 20 000 Jews were arrested. Young Karl Hartland was a Jewish boy living in Essen. His father took him to see the remains of the synagogue which had been set on fire.

Source 12.4 Charles Hannam, 'A Boy in Your Situation', 1977

The front gate was closed and smoke was coming out of the roof . . . Smoke came out of the top windows, and the windows in the room where Karl had had his religious instruction lessons were broken. There was no sign of the fire brigade and a small group of storm troopers stood there looking as if all this had nothing to do with them.

These actions proved beyond doubt that Jews could not expect fair treatment in Germany. Many gave up their homes and moved abroad.

Activities

1 Why were Jews unpopular in Germany even before Hitler came to power? Give three reasons. **(KU)**

2 Read Source 12.1. How can you tell that the author did not like Jews? **(ENQ)**

3 Give two reasons why Source 12.2 is useful evidence about the feelings of Nazis towards the Jews. **(ENQ)**

4 To what extent do Sources 12.3 and 12.4 agree about Nazi treatment of Jewish people? **(ENQ)**

5 Describe actions taken against Jews in Germany after 1933. Mention three actions. **(KU)**

6 If you had been an ordinary German, how would you have felt about these actions?

Racism

The Nazis gloried in being racists. In their programme in 1920 (Source 5.4 p. 26) they had declared that only those of German blood should be allowed to be members of the nation. Their ideas of racial character and superiority went much further. Germans were told they were **Aryan** – a pure breed of high quality destined to rule over lesser people (*Untermenschen*) like the Slavs of eastern Europe, Jews and black people. To maintain their superiority, they had to maintain the purity of the race.

Source 12.5 Adolf Hitler, 'Mein Kampf'

It is never by war that nations are ruined, but by the loss of their powers of resistance, which are exclusively a characteristic of pure racial blood. In this world everything that is not of sound stock is like chaff.

These teachings were total nonsense, but they were popular. It was comforting for Germans, suffering from humiliation and poverty, to be told they would be a 'master race', commanding respect throughout the world. It was also convenient to blame your troubles on those 'foreigners', the Jews.

Source 12.6 — Pictures from a Biology textbook

'National Comrades'

'Community Aliens'

Once in power, the Nazis set about creating what they called the 'national community'. Those of Aryan blood – the 'national comrades' – were portrayed as healthy, handsome and purposeful; lesser breeds – the 'community aliens' – were shown as weak in mind and body, as you can see in Source 12.6.

Treatment of the Jews

Of all the 'community aliens', the Jews suffered worst under Nazi rule. The Nazi attitude towards the Jews was not new; it had been part of the beliefs of extreme Nationalists for many years. Hitler's writings about them built on racist ideas going back to the 19th Century. Even under the Weimar Republic there had been evidence of anti-Semitism in Germany. Often, immigrant Jews from eastern Europe were deported by the authorities. In 1923, during the inflation, there had been a dreadful riot in Scheunenviertel, a part of Berlin with a high Jewish population.

Source 12.7 — Report in the 'Vossische Zeitung', 6 November 1923

Howling mobs in all the side streets. Looting is going on under cover of darkness. On all sides, the same cry: 'Kill the Jews'. It is inflamed racial hatred, not hunger, that has driven them to looting. If anyone with a Jewish appearance walks past, he is followed by a group of youngsters who pick their moment and then fall on him.

On this and similar occasions the police acted against the rioters. It was different after 1933.

To protect the Aryan race from 'contamination' by Jews, the Nuremberg laws were passed in 1935. Already

GENERAL/CREDIT LEVEL

discriminated against, now the Jews were denied their identity as Germans.

> **Source 12.8** From the Nuremberg laws, 1935
>
> *Marriages between Jews and nationals of German or similar blood are forbidden. A Jew may not be a citizen of the Reich. He has no vote in political matters; he may not fill public office. ... Jews are forbidden to fly the Reich and national flag and to display the Reich colours. They are, on the other hand, allowed to display the Jewish colours. The exercise of this right enjoys the protection of the state.*

These laws defined precisely who were to be regarded as Jews and banned Jews from employing German women of child-bearing age as house servants. 'Aryan' Germans were encouraged to break off all contacts with Jews. The British wife of a German lawyer did not realise their effects at first.

> **Source 12.9** Christabel Bielenberg, 'The Past is Myself,' 1984
>
> *The Nuremberg Laws did not hit me hard until they walked quietly and with dignity across the threshold of my own front door. Professor Bauer looked after our children. I was a little puzzled, and very grateful, that he found time one night to sit with me while Nicholas, our eldest son, tossed with fever.*
>
> *Professor Bauer hesitated before leaving the house and then asked me quietly if I still wished him to attend my family. Still? Why ever not? I knew, doubtless, that he was a Jew. I might not have heard, though, that his Clinic had been threatened with having to close down unless he handed it over to an Aryan colleague. He had received threatening letters bidding him to keep his hands off Aryan children. If I insisted I might get involved.*

Soon, Jews had to mark themselves by wearing yellow stars. Then, in 1937, Jewish men and women whose first names were not obviously Jewish had to add Israel or Sara to them.

> **Source 12.10** Covers of identity cards from Nazi Germany. Above is a normal one and below a Jewish one.
>
>

At first many Jews, especially of the older generation, were unwilling to believe the persecution could last.

Source 12.11 — **Fritz Stern**, 'Dreams and Delusions: the Drama of German History', 1988

Jews were torn between believing atrocity stories about the National Socialists, stories that often tended to paralyse action, and hoping things would improve. Some Jews thought that in time the National Socialists would moderate. Jews could take comfort from the fact that there was so little unprovoked anti-Semitism in 1933. Official boycott actions had indifferent results. Germans continued to flock to Jewish doctors and Jewish lawyers.

They tried to live out the trouble, living as quietly as they could and obeying every new restriction on their lives. Only the violence of 1938 and the concentration camps made them flee. Even then, nearly half of the Jews who had lived in Germany in 1933 stayed in Germany.

This anti-Semitic policy actually damaged Germany as well as the people it was intended to hurt. Many of the Jews who emigrated or who suffered and died in the concentration camps were people whose skills Germany could not afford to lose. Apart from doctors like Professor Bauer, there were many other professional people, including teachers, civil servants and lawyers. Others were business people who were important to the German economy. Germany also lost artists, musicians, writers and scientists, including Albert Einstein. In their haste to destroy the Jews, the Nazis undermined their own efforts to make Germany strong.

What people thought

Most ordinary Germans were not strongly anti-Semitic. They did not take much part in the oppression, though they did little to prevent it or protest against it, except where there was violence. Even then they dared not do too much for fear of what might happen to them.

Source 12.12 — **Report from Germany**, November 1938

The brutal measures against the Jews have caused great indignation among the population. People spoke their minds quite openly, and many Aryans were arrested as a result . . . Many people are looking after the Jewish women and children and have put them up in their homes. Housewives are shopping for the Jewish women, because it is forbidden to sell food to them.

Source 12.13 — **Police report**, 26 November 1938

Some have welcomed the actions taken against the Jews; others watched them calmly; others again are sorry for the Jews, though they do not necessarily express this openly.

GENERAL/CREDIT LEVEL

Activities

1. What arguments did the Nazis use to justify their treatment of Jews and other people? **(KU)**

2. How valuable is Source 12.7 as evidence about attitudes towards the Jews in Germany before the Nazis came to power? **(ENQ)**

3. How far do Sources 12.7 and 12.12 agree about anti-Semitism in Germany? **(ENQ)**

4. To what extent did ordinary people support Nazi policies towards the Jews? You should use evidence from the sources and your own knowledge to reach a balanced conclusion. **(KU)**

5. According to Source 12.11, what was the view of Jewish people to their persecution? **(ENQ)**

Group discussion

Why were the Nazis able to get away with their racist policies in Germany in the 1930s? What does your study of the period tell you about German beliefs and attitudes during the 1930s? **(KU)**

13 Life Under Hitler

The Nuremberg rallies

The Nazis attracted many young men with the glamour of uniforms and parades. These were shown off best in the Party Day rallies in the city of Nuremberg. The first one took place in 1925. Only two years later 20 000 people marched through the city streets to listen to Hitler speak.

Source 13.1 Hitler speaking from the podium at the 1934 rally

As *Führer*, Hitler used these annual rallies to impress the people of Germany and the rest of the world. A young architect, Albert Speer, designed a massive new stadium for the 1934 rally, the first with Hitler as *Führer*.

The designers used every trick they could imagine to make the scene as dramatic as possible. Overlooking the stadium was a huge stone eagle, its wingspan over 30 metres across. The arena was surrounded by hundreds of long red banners, each with the black **swastika** against a white circle in the middle. Around the stadium were anti-aircraft searchlights, their beams used to make columns of light in the night sky.

Party members came from all over Germany. They held rehearsals to make sure all would go smoothly. The rally began with several days of processions, meetings and displays. The displays showed how Hitler was keeping his promise to rebuild the army so that Germany would be great once more. Then came the climax of the rally. On 7 September marching bands led a procession of uniformed SA and SS men, with flags flying and standards held high, to the floodlit stadium. Over 200 000 of them stood in straight lines. First, party leaders like Rudolf Hess excited them with fiery speeches and slogans.

Source **13.3** Tanks and infantry take part in a mock battle at the 1938 rally

Some of these sound ridiculous today. In 1934, in that atmosphere, they thrilled the audience and prepared them for Hitler's entrance.

Source **13.2** From a speech by Rudolf Hess at Nuremberg, 1934

The party is Hitler. Hitler is Germany just as Germany is Hitler. Heil Hitler!

At last, the *Führer's* voice reached them through the loudspeakers. When he told them, 'We are strong and will get stronger!' they roared back '*Sieg Heil* – Hail Victory!', their arms straight in salute.

Rallies like these gave the German people excitement and a feeling of belonging. Those who could not be there heard the speeches on the radio or watched the newsreel film in the cinema. They could share in the atmosphere and feel proud to hear their national anthem again.

Activities

1 Describe what made a Nuremberg rally exciting. Mention three things. **(KU)**

2 In what ways did the Nuremberg rallies show that the army was important in Hitler's Germany? Use two pieces of evidence in your answer. **(KU)**

3 Choose from these statements the one you think best explains what Rudolf Hess meant in Source 13.2. Give a reason for your choice.

◆ Hitler is the ruler of Germany.

◆ Hitler and the German people want the same things.

◆ Hitler is like any ordinary German. **(ENQ)**

4 What does Source 13.3 tell you about the Nuremberg rallies? **(KU)**

5 What do you think was the purpose of holding rallies like these? **(KU)**

F/G LEVEL

GENERAL/CREDIT LEVEL

Militarism

The Nuremberg rallies provide only one example of the ways in which the Nazis gave every part of German life a military look. Discipline was central to the regime, even if it had to be imposed by fear. Organisations used military style uniforms. Almost every month in the year had its festival, complete with military parades. For example, on 30 January there was a celebration of the anniversary of Hitler becoming Chancellor, 1 May saw the 'Day of Labour', and on 9 November the 'old fighters' (*Alte Kampfer*) marched through Munich to recall the failed rising of 1923. At every excuse there was a march past, a torchlight procession or a military display.

Source **13.4**

Motorised parade as Hitler opens a section of the autobahn between Frankfurt and Heidelberg

Source **13.5** SS men on parade at Kreuzberg 1935

The emphasis on military display was matched by a growth in military strength. Hitler completely ignored the military clauses of Versailles. The army of 100 000 men had become 550 000 by 1936 and 850 000 by 1938, with a further 900 000 trained reserves.

Source **13.6**

Year	German military spending 1933–1939 (in millions of Reichsmarks)
1933	1900
1934	1900
1935	4000
1936	5800
1937	8200
1938	18 400
1939	32 200

Here, at least, Hitler was keeping his promise to make Germany strong again. In June 1935 he reached a naval agreement with Britain allowing Germany to build a navy up to 35% of the size of the British navy. It also allowed Germany to begin constructing U-boats. This was a triumph for Hitler. It was the first step towards the promised destruction of Versailles. With a new navy, air force and armoured land forces, he had made Germany strong enough to take the risk of sending troops into the Rhineland in 1936. The failure of Britain and France to resist encouraged him to be even more aggressive in the future.

Employment

The growth of the armed forces helped Hitler to keep another of his promises. Unemployment in Germany fell rapidly as men joined the forces, built tanks, ships and aircraft, or took part in the programme of public works which covered Germany with autobahns, stadia and new government buildings. The unemployment figures were also brought down by the flight of Jews abroad and by the imprisonment of so many people in the **concentration camps**. Yet the figures remain dramatic.

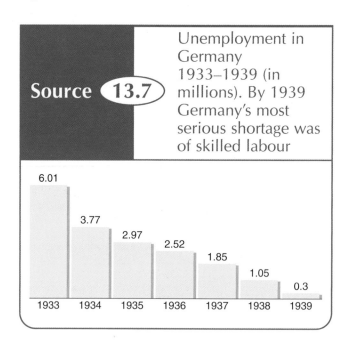

Source **13.7** Unemployment in Germany 1933–1939 (in millions). By 1939 Germany's most serious shortage was of skilled labour

6.01 (1933) 3.77 (1934) 2.97 (1935) 2.52 (1936) 1.85 (1937) 1.05 (1938) 0.3 (1939)

GENERAL/CREDIT LEVEL

GENERAL/CREDIT LEVEL

'Bread and circuses'

It was vital to Hitler that his drive to strengthen Germany should not be ruined by strikes or other labour troubles. Strikes were illegal and the replacement of the unions by the German Labour Front made united action unlikely. Still, to prevent troubles in industry, the Nazis felt it necessary to give the workers some sense of well-being.

Wages were generally slightly higher than they had been under the Weimar Republic, but not enough to guarantee contentment. A special section of the Labour Front was set up to offer encouragement and reward to the workers. 'Strength through Joy' (*Kraft durch Freude or KDF*) offered subsidised package holidays and organised theatre visits, held sports courses and ran outdoor activities. These events became very popular.

Source	13.8	Report to the Social Democratic Party in Exile, 1936

Almost all national comrades rate Strength through Joy as one of National Socialism's really creditable achievements.

I attended a swimming course in which over 50 took part, and I have to admit there was very little party atmosphere. The participants were all ordinary people. There were scarcely any 'Heil Hitlers'. Coming from the old workers' sports clubs as we did, we felt at home, so to speak. It is pretty generally the case now that you can't avoid Strength through Joy if you want to travel to take part in sport. There is simply no other choice.

As well as occupying people's spare time, the Nazis tried to offer them an incentive to work hard. They could join a savings scheme which would give them the chance to own their own 'People's Car', the Volkswagen, which appeared in 1938. In fact, the scheme did not work very well, and few ordinary Germans, if any, claimed their car.

The ultimate public spectacle was the staging of the Olympic Games in Berlin in 1936. Germany prepared to welcome thousands of overseas visitors, determined to show them how good life was under National Socialism. Even anti-Jewish posters were removed while the Games were on.

Source	13.9	'Olympic guests – quick march.' A photomontage by John Heartfield. Dr Goebbels is holding the strings

Der Zweck vons Janze „Olympiagäste, im Gleichschritt – marsch!"

Mit dieser Photomontage kämpfte John Heartfield 1936 gegen die Hitler-Olympiade (Seite 6

Over 100 000 spectators watched the opening ceremony, in which girls dressed in white danced and boys with coloured tunics formed the Olympic rings, while bands played Beethoven's 'Ode to Joy'. The Games were tremendously successful as a publicity exercise, though the rest of the world noted with dismay Hitler's refusal to congratulate black athletes who won medals, especially the star athlete of the Games, American sprinter Jesse Owens. Hitler was so angry when Owens won the 100 metres race that he left the stadium before the medals were presented. He could not accept that one of the lower races (*Untermenschen*) could defeat his Aryan champion.

Activities

1 What evidence is there in Sources 13.4 and 13.5 to support the view that military discipline and symbols were important in Nazi Germany? **(ENQ)**

2 Why was militarism important to Nazi rule in Germany? **(KU)**

3 How did the Nazis try to persuade the German people to support them? **(KU)**

4 a) Was the author of Source 13.8 a Nazi supporter? Give at least two reasons for your answer. **(ENQ)**

   b) Discuss the value of Source 13.8 as evidence of the treatment of ordinary people in Germany. **(ENQ)**

5 How accurate is Source 13.9 as evidence of the way in which the Nazis used the Olympic Games? **(ENQ)**

Propaganda

As John Heartfield's montage suggests, the Nazis used the Olympic Games as an exercise in international propaganda. At home, the Germans were subjected to regular doses of the same medicine.

The parades, the bands and the flags were part of their campaign, but it went much further. From 1933 Dr Goebbels was head of the new Ministry for Public Information and Propaganda. He was well aware of the power of the mass media. Films and newspapers, theatres and radio, magazines and art galleries were all subject to his censorship. The messages they carried all had to reflect the beliefs and values of the Party. The purpose of communication was to carry these beliefs to every German.

Source 13.10 Albert Speer's final speech at his trial at Nuremberg, 1946

His [Hitler's] was the first dictatorship in the present period of technical development, a dictatorship which made complete use of all technical means for the domination of its own country. Through technical devices like the radio and the loudspeaker, 80 million people were deprived of independent thought. It was thereby possible to subject them all to the will of one man.

After 1933 the propaganda message changed. Now that the Nazis were in power there was no need to attack political opponents or to make election promises. Goebbels now had two concerns. First, he had to convince the 'national comrades' of the virtues of living in the National Socialist state. Second, he had to persuade them to participate in the activities of the 'national community' (*Volksgemeinschaft*).

GENERAL/CREDIT LEVEL

Source 13.11 Advertisement – 'All Germany hears the Führer on the People's Receiver'

Economic successes were advertised, along with the virtues of hard work and service. There were successes to celebrate. Not only did unemployment fall, but industrial production increased by 45 per cent in the first two years of Nazi rule and by another 45 per cent in the next three years. Germans were also pleased by the return to Germany of the Saar after a plebiscite in 1935 and by the reoccupation of the Rhineland in 1936.

Hitler claimed to have begun a new social order.

Source 13.12 Hitler speaking in Berlin, 1 May 1937

By my side stand Germans from all walks of life who today are amongst the leaders of the nation: men who once were workers on the land are now governing German states. It is true that men who came from the bourgeoisie and former aristocrats have their place in this Movement. But to us it matters nothing whence they come if only they can work to the profit of our people. We have not broken down classes in order to set new ones in their place; we have broken down classes to make way for the German people as a whole.

At every opportunity examples were shown of people sharing the new national spirit.

Source 13.13 Magazines frequently show how workers spent their breaks 'before' and 'after' 1933

Women in the Third Reich

The Nazis had a great deal to thank women for. During the critical years of 1930–1933, working class women were much less likely than men to vote for the left wing opponents of the Nazis, especially the KPD. In the election of July 1932, in some parts of northern Germany, a higher proportion of women than men voted for the Nazis. It is estimated that throughout Germany 6.5 million women voted Nazi in that election, many of them women who had not voted at all in previous elections. These women did not bring the Nazis to power, but they did help to sustain their political challenge.

Despite this, the Nazis took a very old fashioned view of the place of women in society. Their first economic priority was to reduce male unemployment. One way in which this was achieved was by encouraging women to give up paid work. The Nazis pretended to support equality for women, but in practice this was camouflage for a policy of male domination. As usual, Hitler dressed this up in fancy phrases and flattery.

Source 13.14 Hitler speaking at the 1934 Nuremberg rally

If one says that man's world is the State one might be tempted to say that the world of women is a smaller world. For her world is her husband, her family, her children and her house. But where would the greater world be if there were no one to care for the smaller world?

Put more crudely, women ought to stick to the three Ks: *Kinder, Kirche, Küche* – Kids, Kirk, Kitchen.

Women were discouraged from wearing make up, smoking or buying fashionable clothes. Women were offered rewards for accepting these ideas. Couples getting married could get state loans, but only if the wife gave up her job in a factory or office. An Aryan woman who had four or more children was awarded a medal, the Cross of Motherhood.

In practice, it was impossible for German industry to do without female labour. Although at first the number of women in employment fell, by 1939 37 per cent of women were in work. This was exactly the same proportion as in 1928, the last year before the Great Depression.

Activities

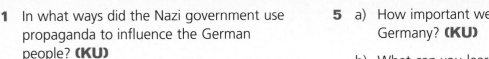

1 In what ways did the Nazi government use propaganda to influence the German people? **(KU)**

2 What is the view of propaganda shown in Source 13.10? **(ENQ)**

3 a) Read Source 13.12. What social change did Hitler claim he had achieved?

  b) What evidence did he present to support his claim? **(KU)**

  c) Do you believe his claims? Give reasons for your answer. **(ENQ)**

4 Are Sources 13.11 and 13.13 more valuable as evidence of life under the Nazis or of Nazi propaganda methods? Explain your answer. **(ENQ)**

5 a) How important were women in Nazi Germany? **(KU)**

  b) What can you learn from Source 13.14 about Hitler's attitude towards the place of women in society? **(ENQ)**

6 'The Nazis made every effort to convince the German people that they were members of a true national community'.

  Describe fully the ways in which the Nazis tried to give German people a good impression of their rule. **(KU)**

  Note: for this answer you should write a short essay of several paragraphs.

14 Young Germany

National socialist youth movements

Hitler claimed that his *Reich* would last for a thousand years. This could only happen if every new generation of Germans became Nazis. For Hitler, this meant that German children must grow up as Nazis. They must believe what Nazis believed. They were to be strong and fit so that boys could grow into soldiers and girls into mothers of the 'master race'. So the Nazis set up organisations to train the children.

FOUNDATION/GENERAL LEVEL

Source 14.1 — **Dr Robert Ley**, a Nazi leader

We start our work when the child is three. As soon as it begins to think, a little flag is put into its hand. Then comes school, the Hitler Youth Movement, the Storm Troop. We never let a single soul go.

Source 14.2 The Führer poses with a young member of the Hitler Youth

84

The Nazis made sure that in school even the youngest children learned only what the Nazis wanted them to learn. They sang Nazi songs in schools decorated with Nazi symbols. To make them fit they took part in physical education and games. They learned about German heroes in history lessons. Even their mathematics problems were based on Nazi ideas. This example reflects the idea that the mentally ill were not fit to be part of the 'master race'.

Source 14.3	Question from a mathematics textbook

A mentally handicapped person costs the public 4 Reichsmarks per day. Within the German Reich, 300 000 persons are being cared for in public mental institutions. How many marriage loans at 1000 Reichsmarks per couple could be paid for each year from the funds spent on these institutions?

Outside school, most children became members of the Nazi youth organisations. At six years old boys joined the *Pimpfen* – 'Little Fellows'. They dressed in uniforms and wore swastika armbands. Before moving up to the 'German Young Folk' (*Deutsches Jungvolk*) when they were 10, the boys had to be able to march, make maps, find direction by the stars and shoot at targets.

When they were 14, the boys went into the *Hitler Jugend* – the Hitler Youth itself. They went camping and played sports. They also practised marching, sang Nazi songs and learned to be loyal to Hitler. As part of their training they were taught to use weapons.

There were also girls' branches of the Hitler Youth. Between 10 and 14 years of age, girls could join the Young Girls'

League (*Jungmädelbund*) and at 15 they moved up to the League of German Girls (*Bund Deutscher Mädel*). They, too, were able to take part in exciting activities.

Source 14.4	'We want to win.' Cover of a magazine of the League of German Girls, March 1939

FOUNDATION/GENERAL LEVEL

Here was the chance of adventure for one 12 year old in 1938.

Source 14.5	**Marianne Mackinnon**, 'The Naked Years', 1987

I was not thinking of the Führer when I raised my right hand, but of games, sports, hiking, singing, camping and other exciting activities. A uniform, a badge, an oath, a salute. There seemed to be nothing to it.

At first, no one *had* to join the Hitler Youth. Many children still belonged to church groups or other organisations. Soon, like the political parties, all other youth organisations were banned or became part of the Hitler Youth. After 1936 children were put under pressure to join and in 1939 it became compulsory. The Hitler Youth had become part of 'national service'.

Activities

1 Why did the Nazis want to control the way in which children in Germany grew up? Give two reasons. **(KU)**

2 What was the Nazi attitude to children according to Source 14.1? **(ENQ)**

3 Describe two ways in which the Nazis tried to influence the way in which children grew up. **(KU)**

4 How far do you agree that the Nazis brought up children to be young soldiers? Use evidence from Sources 14.1 and 14.2 and from your own knowledge to reach a conclusion. **(KU)**

5 Why is Source 14.3 evidence that the Nazis used school lessons for propaganda? **(ENQ)**

6 Compare the evidence in Sources 14.4 and 14.5 about the League of German Girls. In what way do they agree about why girls enjoyed being members? **(ENQ)**

F/G LEVEL

GENERAL/CREDIT LEVEL

Education

Many young Germans became aware of National Socialism at school. It was impossible to avoid: the schools were decorated with Nazi symbols and taught Nazi songs to encourage national loyalty. Their teachers were forced to join the National Socialist Teachers' League, or NSLB (*Nationalsozialistische Lehrerbund*); by 1937 97 per cent of them had become members. Those that the Nazis did not trust because of their political views were sacked. Lessons were to start and finish by giving the Nazi salute and saying '*Heil Hitler!*' Staff and pupils who met in the corridor were supposed to greet each other in the same way. Hitler was clear about the main duty of schools.

Source 14.6 — Adolf Hitler, 'Mein Kampf'

Education is to be the preparation for the later army service. The state must throw the whole weight of its educational machinery, not into pumping children full of knowledge, but in producing absolutely healthy bodies.

As well as preparing young people to be future soldiers of Nazi Germany, Hitler demanded that schools teach – indoctrinate would be a more accurate word – his racist and nationalist beliefs. Young people were not encouraged to think for themselves and make choices but to accept Nazi views and attitudes.

Source 14.7 — National Socialist Teachers' League official, 1937

German youth must be deliberately shaped according to the principles which are recognised as correct and which have shown themselves to be correct: according to the principles of National Socialism.

To achieve these purposes, responsibility for education was taken from the *Länder* and given to a central Ministry for Education and Science. This Ministry redesigned the school curriculum to reflect Nazi beliefs. The Nazi emphasis on physical strength resulted in increased time being given to physical education. Courses and textbooks were rewritten to teach Nazi ideology through lessons in biology (see Source 12.6, p. 71), German language and geography.

History lessons put across the nationalist message by describing Jewish 'crimes', the rise of National Socialism and Germany's soldier heroes. Indeed, the Nazis saw the study of history as having a special place in creating the new national identity.

Source 14.9 — German Central Institute of Education, 1938

The teaching of history must bring the past alive for the young German in such a way that it enables him to understand the present, makes him feel the responsibility of every individual for the nation as a whole and gives him encouragement for his own political activity . . .

The emphasis on military glory in their history lessons fitted well with the children's experience in the Hitler Youth.

GENERAL/CREDIT LEVEL

Source 14.8

A school timetable reflects the military ideal. The heading says, 'The history of the German people is the history of its infantry'

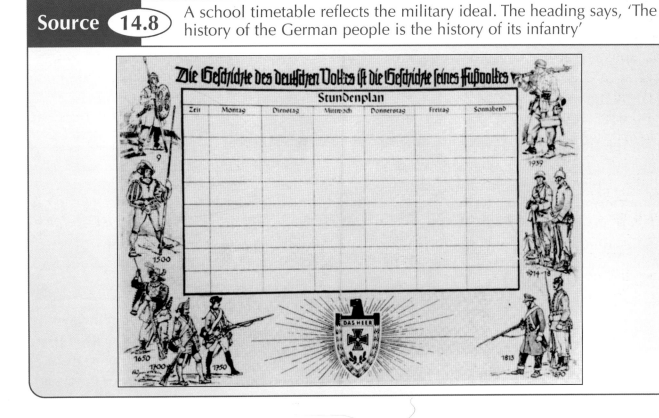

Compulsion

Though many children were attracted by the exciting activities of the Hitler Youth, others wanted to remain members of other youth groups, like the Scouts or the Catholic Youth League, which was strong in Bavaria. Those who resisted the pressure were bullied, even by their teachers. As early as 1933, members of other organisations in at least one town received threatening letters.

Source 14.10

Letter from the Hitler Youth leader, Baldur von Schirach, to members of other organisations in Wiesbaden, 1933.

The Hitler Youth comes to you today with the question: why are you still outside its ranks? We take it that you accept our Führer, Adolf Hitler. But you can only do this if you also accept the Hitler Youth created by him. If you are for the Führer, therefore for the Hitler Youth, then sign the enclosed application. If you are not willing to join the Hitler Youth then write to us on the enclosed blank.*

Given the threat implied by such letters, it is not surprising that membership grew rapidly. Already in 1934 over 3.5 million young Germans between 10 and 18 years old were members of the Nazi youth organisations. By 1938 this figure had doubled, with only 2 million remaining outside. In 1939, 'youth service' became compulsory.

* The blank was a form which father and son had to sign, saying where they worked

Youth activities

Many did not need to be forced to take part. The Hitler Youth offered action, recognition through promotion, feelings of achievement and a sense of belonging.

Source 14.11   Hitler Youth members on parade

Source 14.12

Memoirs of Melita Maschmann, a leader in the Bund Deutscher Mädel

Almost everything took the form of competitions. Not only were there contests for the best performances in sport and at work, but each unit wanted to have the best-kept home, the most interesting travel album, the top collection for the Winter Relief Fund.

Such artificial excitement did not always last. The girl who had been so pleased to join (Source 14.5) lost her enthusiasm when faced with political lectures, endless marching drills and a discipline intended to make everyone the same.

Source 14.13 **Marianne Mackinnon**, 'The Naked Years', 1987

I felt bored with a movement which expected its members to venerate [worship] a flag as if it were God Almighty, and which made me march or stand for hours, listen to tiresome or inflammatory speeches or shout slogans which, somehow, went into one ear and out the other.

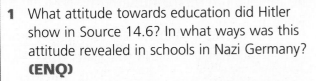

Activities

1 What attitude towards education did Hitler show in Source 14.6? In what ways was this attitude revealed in schools in Nazi Germany? **(ENQ)**

2 To what extent do Sources 14.6 and 14.7 agree about the purposes of education in Nazi Germany? **(ENQ)**

3 What evidence is there in Sources 14.8 and 14.9 that Nazi ideas affected school lessons? Which Nazi ideas do these sources illustrate? **(KU)**

4 Why did membership of Nazi youth organisations grow rapidly during the 1930s? You should use evidence from Sources 14.10, 14.11 and 14.12 and from your own knowledge to reach a balanced conclusion. **(ENQ)**

5 How far do Sources 14.12 and 14.13 give different views about the membership of the Bund Deutscher Mädel? **(ENQ)**

6 'The Nazis looked to the young to guarantee the future of the Third Reich.'

Describe fully the methods used by the Nazis to ensure that the youth of Germany would grow up to support them. **(KU)**

Note: for this answer you should write a short essay of several paragraphs.

Imaginative reconstruction

With your group, use the sources and information in this chapter to make lists of the a) attractive, b) unattractive features of Nazi youth movements. Now write a short play script in which young Germans discuss the Hitler Youth. There should be three characters:

◆ someone who is not a member of the movement

◆ a vigorous supporter who tries to convince the first person to join

◆ a member who has lost his/her enthusiasm and advises against joining.

The play could be performed for the class as an introduction to a discussion on the impact of Nazi youth movements. **(KU)**

GENERAL/CREDIT LEVEL

15 Opposition to Hitler

The working classes

Before Hitler came to power, the Socialists and Communists had been his main opponents. Their organisations, the *Reichsbanner* and the Red Front, had fought street battles against the SA. Surely they could be a focus of resistance?

It was not as easy as that. Following the *Reichstag* fire in 1933, many Communists had been imprisoned (see Chapter 10). The Nazis took all the working-class movements by surprise, so quickly did they act. The main political parties were banned, trade unions made illegal and working-men's clubs shut down. When some groups went underground, systematic raids took place on working-class districts, using the SA, the SS and the Gestapo, as well as the police.

Source 15.1 — Detlev Peukert, 'Inside Nazi Germany', 1987

These planned raids, together with threats, insults, beatings and arbitrary arrests created an atmosphere of helplessness even in working-class strongholds that had until recently seemed to be safe.

Very quickly, even traditional working-class areas were showing their loyalty to the regime, with swastika flags flying from almost every window.

Such organised working-class resistance as did exist took two forms. The Social Democratic Party leaders who escaped arrest by fleeing abroad had information smuggled out to them about life in Germany. These, printed on green paper, were published as the 'green reports', to publicise to the world what was happening. Meanwhile, inside Germany, underground resistance groups cautiously kept in touch with each other to keep their political beliefs alive. They could do little more in the face of the terror inflicted by the Gestapo.

Source 15.2 — 'Hitler calls this LIVING!' by a member of the German Freedom party

Solidarity is growing, but the organisation of fighting groups on anything like a large scale is not yet possible, since the danger of being discovered is still too great.

The activities for children took up almost all spare time they had. Hitler realised he could not win over all members of the older generations, but believed he could gain the total loyalty of the young. As a result they had little time for school homework or to think for themselves about what they wanted to do or become. Children were even used as spies against their own families or teachers. They were expected to report any signs of disloyalty to Hitler or the Reich to the authorities.

Individuals

Though it was impossible to fight Nazism openly, the largest resistance still came from working-class people. This could be as simple as complaining about jobs, food supplies or the cost of living. As early as 1934 Gestapo reports warned about 'grumbling' over issues like food prices, which might grow into revolt.

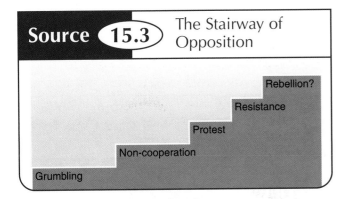

Source 15.3 The Stairway of Opposition

Some went a stage further, by refusing to co-operate. Perhaps they did not send their children to the Hitler Youth, or failed to meet production targets at work. Only a few had the nerve to protest openly, by printing and circulating leaflets, for example. Most of those who had the

courage for such open protests did not remain free for long.

Edelweiss pirates

In the late 1930s, some young people who did not like the military discipline of the Hitler Youth began to meet in groups. Nicknamed 'Edelweiss Pirates' because they often wore metal edelweiss flower badges on their collars, they were really local gangs.

Their main activities were at weekends. They went on camping or hiking trips, sang songs together and simply enjoyed each other's company. Like the hippies of later generations, they wanted freedom from control by authority.

These 'wild' groups saw the Hitler Youth as their enemy and took every opportunity to beat up their patrols. They were not a serious problem for the government, but they could be a nuisance at local level.

Source 15.4 A typical 'wild' group from Köhn (Cologne)

F/G LEVEL

GENERAL/CREDIT LEVEL

Activities

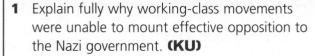

1 Explain fully why working-class movements were unable to mount effective opposition to the Nazi government. **(KU)**

2 How far do Sources 15.1 and 15.2 agree about working-class resistance in Germany? **(ENQ)**

3 In what ways did a) ordinary Germans, b) young people show their disapproval of life under the Nazis? **(KU)**

The Christian Churches Co-operation

Like Socialists, Christians in Nazi Germany faced a difficult time. Many of them shared the Nazis' belief in restoring German strength and their resentment against the terms of the Treaty of Versailles. They soon realised that their leaders' policies of racism and the glorification of war were against Christian teachings of love for other people. Hitler knew this and in a conversation in 1933 with a friend, he said, 'One is either a Christian or a German. You can't be both'. He intended to crush the churches.

Hitler could not afford to attack the churches too quickly. At first, he appeared to encourage them by talking of the importance of moral values. In 1933 he agreed to guarantee the religious freedom of the Roman Catholic Church and its rights in education. In return, the Church promised that its priests would keep out of politics.

Source 15.5 A Nazi funeral in a Protestant Church, 1934

Source 15.6 A Roman Catholic priest shows his acceptance of National Socialism as he returns the salute of a parade of SA members in 1933

To control Protestants, Hitler had Ludwig Müller, a Nazi sympathiser, made Bishop of the Reich. Under his leadership, the 'German Christians' of the **Reich Church**, would be encouraged to co-operate with the Nazis.

Opposition

Despite their agreement, the Nazis sacked Roman Catholic civil servants and tried to shut down their youth organisations and schools. When priests or people complained, they were attacked. Many priests and monks were arrested. In 1937 the Pope issued a statement to be read in churches throughout Germany. In it he spoke of a 'war of destruction' against the Church and urged Roman Catholics to oppose any actions which were against Christian beliefs.

Some Protestant pastors also stood up to the Nazis. In 1934 a former U-boat captain, Martin Niemöller, helped to found the Confessional Church. Members of this church criticised Müller's Reich Church for distorting Christian teaching. Of course, this brought them up against the Gestapo, and many pastors were arrested. Martin Niemöller himself was arrested in 1937 and was held in a concentration camp from 1938 until 1945. Another Protestant academic, Dietrich Bonhoffer, also opposed the Nazis and was arrested and executed.

Hitler made it clear that he would not tolerate opposition, even in the name of God.

> **Source 15.7** Speech by Hitler to the Reichstag, January 1939
>
> *The National Socialist State will ruthlessly make clear to those clergy who, instead of being God's ministers, regard it as their mission to speak insultingly of our Reich. Clergy will be called to account before the Law like any other German citizen. Tens of thousands of clergy fulfil their ecclesiastical duties without ever coming into conflict with the State. The State considers their protection its task. The destruction of the enemies of the State is its duty.*

> **Source 15.8** A Roman Catholic hall after an attack by the SA in 1933

Church resistance to the Nazis was mostly the work of brave individuals, not of proper organisations. Most church members stayed quiet, even loyal to the government, although the Nazis were committing terrible acts of cruelty. Some historians have criticised the churches for failing to speak clearly enough against Nazism, especially over the treatment of the Jews.

Source 15.9 — JRC Wright, Historian

The purpose of the church opposition was self-defence, not a wider, political opposition; the Churches, including the opponents of Nazi policies, frequently affirmed their loyalty to the state and the Führer.

The self-defence was necessary. During the Second World War, Hitler ordered the Bible and Cross to be replaced in German churches with *Mein Kampf* and a sword. As Professor Fritz Stern wrote, 'If Hitler had won the war, he would have attempted to destroy Christianity'.

Activities

1 Describe the ways in which the Nazis tried to control and use the Christian churches. **(KU)**

2 a) How reliable are Sources 15.5 and 15.6 as evidence that Christians in Nazi Germany co-operated with the Nazis? **(ENQ)**

   b) In what way could it be argued that these two sources are biased? **(ENQ)**

3 How accurately does Source 15.7 illustrate Nazi policy towards the Christian religion? **(ENQ)**

4 Look at Sources 15.7 and 15.8. Is there evidence that the Nazis were afraid of the churches? **(KU)**

5 Was opposition from the churches or any groups inside Germany a serious threat to Nazi rule in the 1930s? **(KU)**

Debate

Despite opposition from Socialists, Christians and some ordinary Germans, most Germans were loyal to Hitler, at least in public. There was little organised resistance until Germany suffered the effects of a long, hard war. Why? (KU)

Preparation

In your group, gather evidence to support **one** of the following statements:

There was little open opposition to Nazi rule because:

◆ most Germans agreed with Nazi policies.

◆ the Nazis ruled Germany well.

◆ the Nazis' use of repression made resistance impossible.

◆ the German people were too cowardly to resist.

Write a speech to support the statement you have chosen. The speech should last not more than three minutes.

Debate

One person from each group reads the speech to the class, who take notes of the main arguments, to use later. After all groups have spoken, members of the class speak to support their group's statements or to challenge those of other groups. All points must be supported by evidence, so do not use up **all** of your evidence in your speech. After everyone has had a chance to speak, a class vote may be taken on what was the most important reason for the lack of resistance. You may not vote for your own statement.

16 Postscript: The Road to War

The Treaty of Versailles and the rise of the Nazi Party

The peace treaty that Germany was forced to accept at the end of the First World War shocked and horrified all Germans. The terms of surrender were so harsh many Germans quickly began to think of rejecting them and seeking vengeance on countries such as France and Britain, as you read in Chapter 3.

One result of this anger was that extreme nationalists like Hitler and the Nazis were able to win increasing support from many ordinary Germans and from the army. Hitler made his intentions clear in his book 'Mein Kampf', claiming he would reject the Treaty of Versailles and also obtain living space (Lebensraum) for Germany in Eastern Europe, even at the risk of war.

During the 1930s countries like Britain and France became increasingly convinced that Germany had been too harshly treated at Versailles. They adopted a policy of appeasing Germany, which meant that they tried to take away German resentment by allowing her to remove parts of the treaty seen as unfair. This made Hitler seem successful and increased his support inside Germany.

The 1930s: Nazi Germany and the rest of Europe

Hitler took Germany out of the disarmament conference held in October 1933 and withdrew from the League of Nations, arguing Germany was being treated as a second class nation. Over the next two years Nazi Germany began to rebuild her military might, ignoring the terms of the Treaty of Versailles. Germany secretly increased the number of her aircraft and expanded her army and navy. In March 1935 Hitler declared Germany would no longer be bound by the terms of the Peace Treaty. Three months later Britain showed her willingness to appease Germany by accepting an increase in German naval strength.

In 1936 Hitler took a big gamble when he ordered German troops into the Rhineland, which had been demilitarised in 1919.

Source 16.1 Adolf Hitler, after the German re-occupation of the Rhineland

If the French had then marched into the Rhineland we would have had to withdraw with our tails between our legs, for the military resources at our disposal would have been wholly inadequate for even a moderate resistance.

France and the rest of Europe did not react decisively and the status of Hitler and the Nazi Party was raised in Germany.

Over the next three years Hitler set a series of aggressive foreign policy targets for Germany. In each case he created a crisis in the target country then increased tension by making threats and demands. He prepared for war but hoped he would be successful without fighting.

Source **16.3** **Essay by Theresa Gregory**, a fourth year schoolgirl, 19 September 1938

The Prime Minister did a noble thing in flying to Germany. Even if it did nothing else, it showed the world that Great Britain is striving for peace. Every country in the world applauded his action. The German people themselves have no desire for war. Their reception of Mr Chamberlain, which was very spontaneous and friendly, showed this.

Source **16.2** Map of Hitler's targets

Finally, Hitler decided the rest of Europe wanted appeasement rather than war and invaded the rest of Czechoslovakia in March 1939.

Under Hitler and the Nazis Germany seemed to have regained the power and position she had lost in 1919. Her economy had recovered and many Germans felt that this was also due to the actions of Hitler and his party. In the summer of 1939 Hitler accused the Poles of mistreating Germans in the 'Polish Corridor' and demanded the return of the port of Danzig (Gdansk). Britain and France said that they would declare war on Germany if she attacked Poland.

In 1938 Hitler tricked and bullied Austria into uniting with Germany and the rest of Europe protested but took no other action.

In the same year Germany moved against Czechoslovakia, on the grounds that Germans living under Czech rule in the Sudetenland were being mistreated. Hitler first demanded justice for these Germans then later insisted the Sudetenland be joined to Germany. The leaders of Britain and France, Neville Chamberlain and Edouard Daladier, tried very hard to resolve the crisis Hitler had created and avoid the danger of war.

After their previous failures to act, which he saw as weakness, Hitler thought the Western powers would not live up to their promise to defend Poland, especially after the Soviet Union made an agreement with Germany. On 1 September 1939 his forces launched a blitzkrieg (lightning war) on the Poles. Two days later Britain and France declared war and Hitler had taken Germany into a Second World War.

Activities

1 For what reasons were Germans so strongly opposed to the terms of the treaty of Versailles? **(KU)**

2 Why do you think Hitler followed such an aggressive foreign policy after 1933? **(KU)**

Time Line

Germany	Date	Nazi Party
	1918	
Naval mutinies at Kiel and Wilhelmshaven	**October**	
Abdication of Kaiser; German Republic formed; Ceasefire signed	**November**	
Congress of workers' and soldiers' councils	**December**	
	1919	
Spartacist revolt; elections to National Assembly	**January**	
National Assembly at Weimar	**February**	
Signing of Versailles Treaty	**June**	
New German constitution	**August**	
	September	Hitler joined German Workers' Party
	1920	
	February	National Socialist German Workers' Party programme published
Kapp Putsch	**March**	
Reichstag election	**June**	
	1921	
German reparations bill published	**April**	
	1922	
Assassination of Walter Rathenau	**June**	
	1923	
French and Belgian occupation of the Ruhr	**January**	
Inflation out of control	**Summer**	
Stresemann Chancellor	**August**	
	November	Munich Putsch
	1924	
	April	Hitler's Trial – sentenced to five years' imprisonment
Reichstag election	**May**	'Racialists' win 32 seats
Dawes Plan accepted	**August**	
Reichstag election	**December**	'Racialists' win 32 seats
	1925	
Death of President Ebert	**April**	
Hindenburg elected President	**May**	
	August	First Nuremberg Rally
Locarno Treaty	**December**	
	1926	
Germany invited to join League of Nations	**September**	

Germany	Date	Nazi Party
	1928	
Reichstag election	**May**	Nazis win only 12 seats
	1929	
Young Plan proposed	**June**	
Death of Gustav Stresemann	**October**	
Wall Street Crash leads to recall of American loans and the start of rising unemployment		
	1930	
Brüning Chancellor	**March**	
Reichstag election	**September**	Nazis win 107 seats
	1932	
Hindenburg re-elected President	**April**	Hitler takes Hindenburg to a second ballot
Von Papen Chancellor	**May**	
Reichstag election	**July**	Nazis win 230 seats
Reichstag election	**November**	Nazis win 196 seats
Von Schleicher Chancellor	**December**	
	1933	
	January	Hitler Chancellor; two other Nazis in the Cabinet
Reichstag fire	**February**	Decree for the Protection of People and State gives Hitler emergency powers
Reichstag election	**March**	Nazis win 288 seats; Enabling Act passed
SPD banned; other parties dissolved	**June**	Nazis replace members of other parties in the Cabinet except Von Papen
	July	Nazi party the only legal party in Germany
	1934	
	May	Trade Unions replaced by German Labour Front
	June	'Night of the Long Knives'
Death of Hindenburg	**August**	Hitler declared *Führer*
	1935	
Anglo-German naval agreement	**June**	
	September	Nuremberg Race Laws issued
	1934	
Re-occupation of the Rhineland	**March**	
Berlin Olympic Games	**August**	
	1938	
Anschluss with Austria	**March**	
Munich agreement over Czechoslovakia	**September**	
	November	*Kristallnacht*: destruction of Jewish property
	1939	
Occupation of Czechoslovakia	**March**	
Invasion of Poland; outbreak of WWII	**September**	

Glossary

Appeasement
Foreign policy followed by Britain in the 1930s under Prime Ministers Stanley Baldwin and Neville Chamberlain. It involved allowing Germany to re-arm, unite with Austria, and invade Czechoslovakia – largely because of the harsh treatment of Germany under the Treaty of Versailles and because people in Britain were strongly against another war.

Aryan
Sanskrit (Indian) word meaning 'noble'. Hitler used the idea of a pure, healthy, noble (Aryan) German race to justify attacks on Jews (anti-Semitism) and anyone who opposed the Nazi Party. Only true Aryans belonged in Hitler's Germany.

Bolshevik
Communists who seized power in Russia in 1917.

Clemenceau, Georges
Became Prime Minister and Minister for War in France in 1917. Organised French contribution to victory over Germany in 1918. Demanded harsh treatment of Germany at peace negotiations and quarrelled with Lloyd George and Woodrow Wilson over the peace terms.

Concentration camps:
First used by British in South Africa during the Boer Wars but widely employed by the Nazi party from 1933 to hold political opponents and Jews without trial and often in the harshest of conditions.

Dawes Plan
American plan meant to help Germany recover from inflation and economic collapse by reorganising reparation payments and removing Allied troops from the Ruhr industrial area of Germany. Worked well, though opposed by Hitler, but had to be replaced by another American strategy, the Young Plan, in 1929 following the international economic collapse caused by the Wall Street Crash.

Ebert, Freidrich
Leader of the Socialist SPD party in Germany. Supported the war and became Chancellor when the Kaiser abdicated. President of the post-war Weimar Republic and very unpopular for ending the war and accepting the Treaty of Versailles. Died 1925.

Gestapo (SS)
Formed as the state secret police in Prussia by Hermann Goering in 1933. Became the Schutzstaffel (SS) in 1934, controlled by Reinhard Heydrich and Heinrich Himmler and provided Hitler's personal bodyguard. Members had a distinctive black uniform with a silver skull badge. Had over 50 000 members and about 160 000 other agents. Used to identify and eliminate opponents of Nazi ideas in Germany and elsewhere.

Goebbels, Dr. Josef
Academic and writer. Joined Nazi party in 1926 and was a strong admirer of Hitler. Not a typically true German in appearance, being very small and dark. Responsible for propaganda for the Nazis from 1933.

Goering, Hermann
German air ace during First World War. Wounded in Munich Beer Hall Putsch in 1923 and fled to

Sweden. Returned to Germany and became a member then President of the *Reichstag* in 1932. Became Minister for the Interior and head of the armed forces under Hitler. Responsible for violent attacks on Communists and Jews whom he saw as major opponents of the new Nazi Germany. Committed suicide 1946.

Hitler, Adolf
1889–1945. Born in Austria. His family was quite well off and expected Adolf to be successful. Intelligent, popular pupil at primary school but he did not complete secondary education. Went to Vienna to study art but could not get admission to art college. Tried unsuccessfully to join Austrian army but did manage to enlist in German army after war broke out in 1914. In 1919 became involved as spy for army investigating revolutionary groups in Germany. Became leading member of the German Workers' Party largely because their ideas on nationalism and racism were like his own. In 1920 he renamed it the National Socialist Workers' Party of Germany and the Nazi Party was born.

Inflation
This happens when prices rise rapidly and the government tries to reduce problems facing people by printing more paper money. This in turn pushes prices and wages up further. In Germany during 1923 prices, wages and the amount of paper money in circulation rose so rapidly it was called 'hyper-inflation' and German banknotes lost all value.

Kaiser
Emperor Wilhelm II.

League of Nations
International organisation set up after World War I to try to prevent further wars by encouraging countries to discuss international problems and disputes and to agree to reduce the strengths of armies and navies or face economic sanctions.

Ludendorff (General)
Successful German general, believed in need to fight war on land and sea and thus partly to blame for entry of America into war against Germany.

Prussia
An old kingdom and one of the most important founding parts of the German empire.

Reich Church
Nazis did not trust churches, Catholic or Protestant. In 1933 Hitler made and agreement (Concordat) with the Pope allowing Catholics to worship freely as long as priests and others did not interfere with his plans for Germany. All Protestant churches were united under the control of Ludwig Muller as Bishop of the Reich. Churchmen from all faiths did oppose Hitler and many died as a result.

Rohm, Ernst
A major in the German army, he was responsible for Hitler's work as spy in 1919. Persuaded by Hitler to join German Workers' Party then Nazi Party. Dismissed from army in 1923 because of his involvement with Hitler in Munich Putsch and left Germany. In 1931 Hitler recalled him to be leader of the S.A. (Brownshirts), which he quickly made into a strong military force. Hitler was persuaded by Himmler and Goering that Rohm was a danger to his leadership and, reluctantly, ordered him executed during the Night of the Long Knives.

Spartacists
Named after the slave Spartacus who led a revolt against the Romans in 73 BC Extreme group, originally founded by Rosa Luxemburg and Karl Leibknecht in 1915 as an anti-war movement.

Swastika

Very old symbol of life and good luck. Like 'Aryan' the word is from Sanskrit and the swastika cross is found all over the world from as early as 3000 years ago. In the late 19th century it was used as a symbol of German nationalism and in 1920 Hitler adopted it for the new Nazi party.

Wall Street Crash

American stock market crash: in 1929 a financial panic hit the US Stock Market on Wall St., New York. Companies collapsed, shares lost all their value, and millions of people lost jobs and savings. The effects were felt all over the world, especially in European countries like Germany. The result was a major economic depression which caused many to turn to the Nazis to save Germany.

Wilson, President Woodrow

American leader, a Democrat and reformer. In 1914 he did not want America involved in a European war but by 1917 had changed his view and not only lead America into the war but organised the war effort very vigorously and efficiently. Came to Europe in 1919 determined to establish a lasting peace through a League of Nations.

Internet Resources

In the course of revising this series of books it became obvious that there is an extensive range of excellent resource materials freely and readily available on the Internet for students and teachers alike. The range includes photographs and maps, video, text, simulations, sample questions and answers. In addition, there are sites offering help with the use of source extracts, other documents and different primary materials.

What follows is not offered as a complete or even comprehensive list of relevant sites but does represent valuable, interesting and enjoyable additional ways of learning about the past. Nor are the sites sorted by level. Several cover more than one context and these are listed first as general resources while others are under more specific headings.

No problems were encountered in using the sites in the list but, as with all internet sites, adverts and pop ups can turn up, sometimes because the site has used sponsors to pay for its place on the internet. The publisher and authors take no responsibility for the appearance of such unlooked for intrusions. Please do type web addresses carefully and, if any unwelcome pop ups etc. do appear, close them immediately or they may be repeated or even freeze up your screen.

Sites covering several contexts/topics

www.bbc.co.uk/education/history
A very wide and easily accessible set of resources covering mainly British history, using video, photographs, documents, timelines, biographies and including the two World Wars. An easy site to find your way around.

http://www.bbc.co.uk/history/scottishhistory/
Well organised resources for ancient and modern Scotland and including links to film archives in a media museum.

www.spartacus.schoolnet.co.uk/
Offers very easily accessed resources for British, European and American history and encourages an on-line interactive approach with newsletters on learning and teaching history.

www.schoolshistory.org.uk
This site is produced by Laisterdyke H.S. Bradford and is designed to help students and teachers plan history revision on a number of British, European and other topics. The site also encourages teacher and student interaction and lists several other history sites and search engines for finding information. It is supported by the use of adverts.

www.schoolhistory.co.uk
Produced by Neale-Wade Community College, Cambridgeshire. Comprehensive range of (revision) resources, at different levels, on British, European and American topics, plus links to other relevant sites.

www.historylearningsite.co.uk
British and European history at various levels, using text, photographs and some short videos.

www.learningcurve.pro.gov.uk
Public Record Office site for students and teachers, resources for British history such as documents, visuals and video and with links into a number of other useful history sites.

www.historygcse.org.
Well organised site, for teachers and students, with resources for European and American topics and numerous links to other sites and revision materials.

Specific sites 1890–1945

www.firstworldwar.com
Very straightforward site providing documentary and visual materials in an easily accessible manner with no frills.

www.bbc.co.uk/history/war/wwone
Very comprehensive site including primary sources of many types, video, poetry, local information.

www.pro.gov.uk/pathways/firstworldwar
Public Record Office site on World War I, containing wide range of documentary and photographic resources, well organised and accessible.

www.bbc.co.uk/history/war/wwtwo
Very comprehensive site on World War II, with written, photographic, video and audio resources and links to other sites and topics – such as propaganda, Hitler.

http://www.bbc.co.uk/schools/gcsebitesize/history/germany1919to45
Mainly intended for revision but with guidance on topics such as Germany 1919–1923, Weimar Germany, Hitler's rise to power, Hitler and Nazism, the Nazi state, source evaluation.

There are many, many other sites which can be accessed using a search engine like Google, to find topics as general as World War One, votes for women or as specific as the Somme, Emmeline Pankhurst. There are also valuable sites produced by schools, to make best use of research done by teachers and pupils. Two examples are given below.

http://www.ellonacademy.org.uk/
Follow the site map to the history department for resources and links to other sites.

www.passmores.essex.sch.uk/
Follow the site map to humanities and then to history for resources and links to other sites.

Index